Ms.
Means
Myself

By the same author . . .

Does Anyone Here Know God?
Honey for a Child's Heart
The Christian Way of Death

Ms. Means Myself

by GLADYS HUNT

ZONDERVAN PUBLISHING HOUSE
OF THE ZONDERVAN CORPORATION
GRAND RAPIDS, MICHIGAN 49506

Second printing December 1972
Third printing May 1973
Fourth printing October 1973
Fifth printing December 1973
Sixth printing January 1974

Printed in the United States of America

To Keith

who has provided the climate
for my fulfillment

Contents

Preface

Writing a book about women and for women takes a good bit of courage. Women have always been a lively subject, but smoldering feelings have burst into real fire today and almost everyone willingly shares a strong opinion with nearly evangelistic zeal.

Taking a vote on opinions says little about their validity, however. Background, temperament and life situations produce a variety of prejudices and "convictions." And it is this that makes writing a book on so volatile a subject a hazardous experience. The important thing is to see the big picture beyond one's own emotional horizons — to observe principles at work in the world, to insist on what is just and right while avoiding the enticements that only hurl one over a cliff, and to relate small or large satisfactions to what is ultimately the meaning of life.

I do not expect everyone to agree with all of my conclusions, but I do expect that those who discuss it will have both the courtesy and integrity to read *all* of the book rather than selected chapters. What I have written comes out of years of friendship and counseling with women in real life situations — in the student world, in rural communities, in suburbia and in a university community.

It is true that I write from a given set of presuppositions. Everyone who opens her mouth to speak or picks up her pen to write does so. In a day when many espouse the autonomy of mankind, I speak from a markedly different point of view. I believe God has revealed Truth to us which cannot be ignored, and that he is actively involved in our world. Though God exists apart from his universe, he is not divorced from it. He has communicated with us. He continues to intervene; he is the initiator in our lives. He has created us and everything he has communicated indicates that he desires our highest good. The Bible contains the principles which govern our conduct and illumine our nature. I take seriously the moral bankruptcy of mankind apart from God and the necessity of redemption. I write from these convictions.

I accept biblical revelation along with the responsibility for its careful interpretation. Throughout this discussion I have tried to handle both the undergirding principles found in Scripture and the specific teaching of biblical passages with integrity. The rules of biblical interpretation require that we give any passage the obvious meaning the author intended in the context in which he writes. Secondly, Scripture must interpret Scripture. We do not find truth when we set out to prove our point of view or use proof texts out of context. Specifically it is difficult to approach Paul's words about the role of women in the church with openmindedness. Too much teaching has already conditioned us on these passages. What is the real life situation to which Paul spoke? What should be its primary interpretation on this basis? What is the weight of Scripture on this subject? It is here that we all need a good deal of humility and willingness to learn.

The larger issues are those of becoming whole persons, human beings who know the meaning and beauty of life, who maximize their potential, who do not exploit others to their advantage, and who have learned that godliness, with contentment, is great gain.

I am indebted to my husband for his encouragement in the rigors of writing a book which could so easily promote debate rather than decision. And I am thankful for the prayers of my family and friends and for the loving help of Jane Richardson in the preparation of the manuscript.

GLADYS M. HUNT

1

Call Me Ms

Ms has been called an abbreviation in search of a word. But a look in the dictionary shows MS or ms, variously capitalized or uncapitalized, represents many words already found. Manuscript. Main Switch. Millisecond. Margin of Safety, Metric System, Multiple Sclerosis, Maximum Stress. It's a long list. And one editor added another: Militant She.

Direct mail experts are happy with the Women's Lib move to use Ms as a designation for a female person without specifying her marital status. Mr. for male; Ms. for female. It cleans up a mailing list and takes away the uncertainty of whether she is married or unmarried when addressing correspondence. Ms is in, a popular subject for quip-writers for a while, but eventually a quiet new mark on the history of women.

More profoundly for each woman Ms means My Self. What is your view of your self? Nothing is as great an impediment to getting along with others as being ill at ease with yourself. Self-acceptance is crucial to accepting others, and it is a necessity for living with yourself. It is not humility that makes a person exclaim, "I don't like me!" or "I can't do it." It is rather a destructive root of unbelief about self and personal worth.

Robert Frost once said it another way. He said, "No one scares me so much as someone who is scared." Essentially Frost is describing the way a negative cycle is set in action. Another's fear binds me in some peculiar way and I react, instead of acting as a free agent. Suddenly I lack spontaneity. His self-consciousness makes me self-conscious, and I must struggle to free myself from the web of his restraint.

The person who cannot accept herself sets in motion myriads of negative cycles. Because she has sent out negative impulses, the impulses she receives confirm her view of herself.

Negative people are hard to live with, no matter who they are. If you have ever met Eeyore, the gray donkey, from the Winnie-the Pooh stories, then you'll know what I mean. Eeyore lives in a gloomy corner among the thistles of the Hundred Acre Woods because he is a gloomy character. When Pooh says, "Good morning to you, Eeyore," he replies, "Good morning to you, too, Pooh. If it *is* a good morning. Which I doubt." He rarely takes any positive action toward others, and is almost accusative when someone acts positively toward him. He adds hilarity to the stories because of his ridiculous self-consciousness and the ludicrous postures others take to reassure him of his worth. When we read about Eeyore everyone laughs because we *know* people like this!

In this way, people with low esteem seem to live against others, rather than for others. When this kind of person enters a room full of people, she automatically assumes no one will like her. Or perhaps *certain* people will not like her. She projects her view of her self onto others. Her chances for natural friendship are gone before she begins. Entering with a negative idea, she proceeds to collect available data to confirm her self-view. Negative feelings take on many hues. *He will not find me interesting. I am not a good conversationalist. Everyone is more smartly dressed than I am.* The list is as varied as any person's insecurities.

There is another way to live defensively. Instead of concluding, "They will not like me," a person crashes into situations with the foregone conclusion, "I will probably not like them." It's a cover-up for expecting rejection. And it probably means that the person has never learned to trust anyone in all her life!

Whatever the mode, whatever the cause, the end result is a terrible kind of slavery to self. Low self-esteem usually has roots in our past: rejection by someone important at a critical stage in life; love given as a reward for performance; a repressive life-style during childhood; comparisons within a family; family status in a community — all can produce a pattern of internalizing or living warily in relationship to others. When the antenna is always out to bounce off others we take our self-view from how others react to the signals sent out. Which is a disastrously self-defeating process.

Society's pressures heighten a sense of worthlessness. Knowledge increases so rapidly; we can never know all there is to know nor keep up with new trends, new ideas or even a current vocabulary. "What's in" can drive anyone looking for security by being "with it" to utter despair. The consumer rage, "You'll keep him if you use. . . . product," or "Be successful, try. . . ." undercut any simple sense of security. A person can begin to feel, "There is no place for me."

Add to this all the trivia published on women today, and you've entered into a cult of feminine uncertainty. To wear ruffles or to strive to be president of the company — or both? On one page of a journal is an article about the kind of women men like; on the next page is a stirring assault on male chauvinism. One psychiatrist writes about bargaining with your children and not repressing their independent spirit. In another magazine of the same month a study commission reports on permissive parenthood and its effect on juvenile delinquency. One article shouts out *Who Needs Men?* And another tells you how to capture one and get him to the altar.

But it's not womanhood that is basically at stake here; it is personhood. The struggle to accept one's self and have some identity is the cornerstone for building a meaningful life. We must come to terms with personal worth. Who can tell us who we are and what we are worth?

God can. He is the major presupposition on which this book is built. In the final analysis, his is the only opinion that counts. He is the Creator and Sustainer of the universe. He *is* the ground of our being. He is the all-powerful, all-knowing, ever present Love. He is ultimate Reality. He is the perfection of fatherhood. And he has told us about our value; his actions have demonstrated our worth; his daily concern verifies our personhood. *Who* we are is best defined by *Whose* we are. Discomfort and unrest fade when we know God as Father.

We have grown used to the phrases of men which define value. *Her father is worth a million dollars. She has made worthwhile contributions in that field.* The crowd-stoppers, the celebrities, the producers. These are worthwhile. And then some scientific buff tells us that the chemical value of a person is $1.40. Inflation. It used to be 98 cents.

The fact is that the world's standard of worth has become so much a part of our thinking that we have trouble hearing and understanding what God is really saying to us about our value in his sight. God has openly declared our personal worth at Calvary. To question his declaration is unbelief, not humility.

Everyone needs to visit Calvary for two reasons: 1) to see the awfulness of our personal sin that necessitated the death of Christ and 2) to see that God thought we were worth dying for. Both are necessary if we are to understand anything about God's love. Emphasizing either one to the exclusion of the other weakens the value of the one. Understanding both is to comprehend the good news of the Gospel.

Many people have just enough religion to make them miserable. They believe in a God who takes sin seriously, who has reminded mankind of moral failure, but they stop there. Keenly aware of inadequacy, they live in the slough of despond — worthless, sinful, guilty. They find no comfort in God for their lack of self-acceptance. His verdict only confirms that they already know about themselves. They may say they believe their sins can be forgiven, but God's love is conditional. It is based on an *if*. *If love* allows people to experience little freedom from their feeling of inadequacy. They are more conscious of themselves than of God.

Ellen had this kind of a problem. She had recounted a troubled childhood to me. Her mother died when she was fourteen and an overly busy father took over the reins of the household. No one had time to listen to Ellen's needs or to understand her loneliness. So she sought comfort elsewhere with older boys who claimed to love her, but who only used her. Each time she felt the ashes of no love, of exploitation, and declared it would never happen again. But her personal need made her vulnerable in this area.

During her freshman year at university she met a girl who told her about God's love and forgiveness. It was bigger than anything Ellen could ever imagine and she hungered to know God and be loved by him. She spoke of her faith in Jesus Christ and of God's forgiveness. But in reality it was a long time before she *really* accepted the forgiveness God offered her. Her sins were always before her. She needed constant reassurance from others as to the value of her person. Fear that she might slip again plagued her. Then she would lose God, too.

Often this kind of misery over self is found in homes or churches where strong teaching about sin is regular fare but where the freedom Christ offers is seldom mentioned. The psychological bent of a person may cause her to hear only verses that speak of "denying yourself" or "hating your own life" or "in my flesh dwells no good thing." These phrases feed an already developed low self-esteem and are taken out of context to add to her woe.

Phillips Brooks once said, "The true way to be humble is not to stoop until you are smaller than yourself, but to stand at your real height against some higher nature that will show you what the real smallness of your greatness is." I like that. It is true to the teaching of the Bible. God has declared our value, our personal worth. He created us with our present genes; he can redeem all of the experiences that make our life. So stand up tall; give him all that you are. We do not need to fuss over ourselves. Boasting is excluded when one is in proper relationship with God.

Others progress a step further. They know God loves them and has accepted them, but are quite sure that he loves them *because* they have trusted him and *because* they do their very best to be as good as possible. *Because love* is risky. Given an imperfect action and the love disappears. But even worse is the high standard of performance for the wrong reason. He loves *because*. People caught in this trap usually come from backgrounds where love is given on the basis of performance, and withheld if there is disapproval.

I am increasingly convinced that a major cause of the despondency, the ineffectual living, the lack of freedom, the feeling of worthlessness so common in today's world is a failure to understand what God has done in redeeming us — and how and why he has done it.

Recently I heard of a postage stamp that was auctioned off for $78,000. It was a small piece of paper scarcely ¾ of an inch by an inch. I would never have paid such a price for such a thing! But its value did not depend on my feelings. Its value was found in the heart of the man who was willing to pay such an enormous price for it.

Just so our value does not lie in our own feelings. It lies in what one is willing to pay to redeem us. God declared our value at Calvary. Your value. My value. He said openly, "I think you are worth dying for!" God said that. If you doubt your own worth, you are disputing the God who made you.

That's the good news the Christian has to share. You are loved. God loves you. He sent his Son to Calvary to take care of your sin problem — the sins which make God seem so far away from you. God offers to save you from your sin, your self, your inadequacies, your depressions — because he loves you. He offers this redemption as a free gift, but a gift has to be received to be a valid gift. And receiving this gift involves a personal confrontation with the living God. Being a Christian is not merely believing a set of truths or being a moral church-goer. It is establishing a relationship with the God who loves you, who has designed you to live in fellowship and harmony with himself.

God means for his children to live with an enormous sense of well-being. He made it possible for us to be free from all our old hang-ups and the opinions that bind us. He constantly assures those who trust him of his steadfast love. "You shall be mine, says the lord of hosts, in the day when I make up my jewels." He calls us his children, and we enter into the wonder of the Fatherhood of God. He promises his continued presence with us. "I will never leave you nor forsake you." He tells us not to be anxious because he knows all our needs. His resources are available to us as we trust him. Those who come and eat at his table are satisfied.

The Apostle Paul demonstrates this as he writes from prison, "Rejoice in the Lord always." His letters ring with a sense of well-being. Yes, he is conscious of sin. He described himself as the chief of sinners, but quickly he went on to rejoice in the deliverance of the Lord. Yes, he was pressing on to the prize of the high call of God in Jesus Christ but not because God's love was dependent upon his striving. God's love was his source of joy and freedom even in prison. He declared that we are more than conquerors through him who loved us.

What we are getting to now is a basic understanding of what justification is all about. *Justification* is one of the most important concepts in the Bible. It is not a word common to our vocabulary and needs explanation. Translators of modern English editions have struggled to find an adequate synonym and have failed. A word study of justification requires paragraphs if we are to comprehend its marvelous truth. Translating the word with the phrase "put right with God" conveys only part of the truth.

Salvation means being justified. *Justifictaion* is a declaration by God; it is a legal act. *We are declared righteous by God.* It is not something that results from what we do, but rather something that is done to us. God regards us as righteous the moment we exercise faith. Furthermore, he declares us righteous even though we deserve his wrath. We bring no goodness to him which makes his declaration necessary. No, he acts on our behalf because of Calvary. The only action we can take is one which makes it personally effective for us — our individual faith.

Often when a question is asked about the meaning of justification, someone will define it *Just-as-if-I'd never sinned.* That's a neat little handle, but like many simplifications it doesn't convey the whole truth. It is as inadequate in defining God's action toward us as the house, swept clean but left empty mentioned in Jesus' parable. God does not treat us simply as if we had never sinned but, deserving his wrath, *he gives us his righteousness.* Not a slate wiped clean, but inscribed with the righteousness of Jesus Christ.

Furthermore, justification does not mean that we are made righteous in the sense that we are not longer conscious of sin. Justification makes no actual change in us; it is a declaration by God concerning us. Failure to understand this puts people on a spiritual roller coaster and our misunderstanding is the devil's hey-day.

On any given day you may be conscious of failure, of having disappointed yourself and God. You find yourself thinking, *Now I've done it. God has turned his back on me. In fact, I am going to have a hard time restoring his approval of me."* And if you believe that, you turn to wallow in your failures, knowing discouragement and defeat. You are sure you are going to have to do penance or work very hard at the Christian life to be acceptable again. It's the devil's lie.

Your *condition* does not yet conform to your *position.* Your position, if you are a Christian, is this: *declared righteous by God.* The whole process of the Christian life is to grow, to change so that our condition is more and more conformed to our position in Christ. The Bible calls this sanctification.

That is why it is so important to understand justification. Doubts come about ourselves. We must turn from ourselves to see God's verdict. Yes, he has pronounced us guilty. We do not take this lightly. "The wrath of God is revealed from heaven against all unrighteousness" (Romans 1:18). But God has done something about our guilt.

We see both his justice and his love at Calvary. And we read and believe one of the most important verses in the Bible: "They are justified by his grace as a gift through the redemption which is in Christ Jesus" (Romans 3:24). Declared righteous by faith.

If God accepts us, are we not insulting him to fail to accept ourselves? "Being justified we have peace with God," Paul writes in Romans 5:1. Why not peace with ourselves as well?

I am not talking about an egotistic self-love; I am talking about the kind of self-acceptance that affirms our personal worth and frees us from the prison of self-absorption. When we need constant reassurance about our personhood, we have set self in the center. The Psalmist reveals the secret to mental, spiritual and physical health so beautifully: "I keep *the Lord* (not self) always before me; because he is at my right hand, I shall not be moved. Therefore my heart is glad and my soul rejoices; my body also dwells secure" (Psalm 16:8, 9). Notice that the heart, the soul and the body — the whole person — is affected by this perspective.

Our problem with reflecting on self is that our thoughts either lead us to self-praise and self-satisfaction or plunge us into discouragement and despair. Whichever it may be, inevitably any view of God is shut out and we lose the wonder of being justified. When we get hold of what it cost God to justify us, and the love that led him to do it, our self view takes on biblical perspective. God has redeemed us; we can lift up our heads and shout praises. God's love is an *in-spite-of kind of love* — the kind of love that is safe, that lets us dump our load honestly before him, assured of his constancy.

Why is justification so important to understand? Because it is the only worthy ground of our own self-acceptance. Your family may have given you an adequate self-concept by their support of your personhood, whether they claim to know God or not. But the spring of their ability to do that is the love of God revealed in Christ even though they do not know this. In contrast, you may come from a scarred background. Whether your battle in self-acceptance will ultimately be easier or harder than the person from a secure background depends on your openness to receive and believe. Perhaps you will appreciate the value of justification more fully because you are more desperate to do so. But regardless of background, God offers us the freedom of knowing our personal worth is bound up in his character. He believed we were worth dying for; he declares those who believe justified!

> *They are justified by his grace as a gift through the redemption which is in Christ Jesus.*
>
> Romans 3:24

This verse is like John 3:16 in conveying the message of our salvation. We have already spoken of the meaning of being justified. Notice other important words in the verse: grace, gift, redemption. All three words indicate that we have done nothing to deserve being declared righteous or justified. It comes to us freely, as a gift of God, in response to our faith. Not everyone receives the gift, but those who believe are justified. Grace is a wonderful word! Grace is the exercise of the spontaneous love of God. Though we deserve his wrath, he chooses to give us his love. Notice that it is *his* grace. Grace only comes from the heart of God. But it cost God something — *the redemption which is in Christ Jesus.* Because God is holy and just, something had to happen before our forgiveness could become possible. Our sins were paid for by the death of Christ. He ransomed us. Our redemption came to us through Christ Jesus. Thus, Paul goes on to say, God proves himself to be both just and the justifier of all who believe in Jesus.

Understanding this led Martin Luther to pen,

> Lord Jesus, thou art my righteousness
> I am thy sin;
> Thou hast taken upon thee what was mine,
> Thou hast set upon me what was thine;
> Thou hast become what thou wast not
> That I might become what I was not.

This is what it means to be made free. "For freedom Christ has set us free," Paul wrote to the Galatian Christians. God wants us to be free to be who we really are. Yet so few have entered into his freedom. Meeting a woman who is genuinely free to be herself, with her hangups dumped at the foot of the cross and acting without self-consciousness, is so rare an experience that it scares some people into a corner. Such a woman is the norm for Christian womanhood. She may not be average, but she is normal. And God wants to raise our averages.

What is such a woman free to do? She is free to love God. She is free to love others. Appreciating that God took the initiative in our redemption — and keeps on taking the initiative in individual lives — she is free to follow his example. She reaches out to others on the basis of love, not only need. She is free to forgive because she knows herself forgiven. She accepts herself because God has accepted her.

Lacking this freedom, some women are like tightly closed buds, atrophying on the vine. Afraid to open up, they do not dare risk the bloom lest it be less beautiful than someone else's.

Others become harping critics, quick to point out error in someone else and slow to love. Others don't criticize, they just internalize, never letting anyone know who they really are. They don't risk exposure or love or acceptance. Some play games, wearing the mask of a role they have chosen, sometimes a very spiritual role. Those are outwardly pious and inwardly barren, still unknown to anyone else or themselves. Others talk too much, skirting all the issues which might reveal their real person. And still others become authorities on any subject, even Biblequoters, to hide blatant insecurities.

Increasingly women are trying to prove their personal worth by achieving in the market place of the world. Honors, paychecks, positions, beauty — any bid for recognition can soothe the nagging doubt and keep us from facing ourselves. It is at this very point that the contemporary Women's Liberation Movement may lead us astray. I am a feminist when issues of fair opportunity, employment and paychecks are at stake. The creation mandate to "subdue the earth" was given to both female and male, and vocationally there should be no closed doors for women who have the ability and the calling to pursue a given field of study. But when all the doors are open, we will still have the human problem of personal worth. We are not equally gifted; we do not have equal opportunities even within our own ranks. Each woman is different. The woman who possesses the epitome of what other women long for still faces her lonely, uncertain self.

To define our worth by giving us new things to do, better jobs or larger paychecks is still to miss the heart of our need. Our worth is not bound up in the position we hold, what we do or what we own. That may only be a new kind of bondage, fraught with competitiveness and comparisons.

We make our own prisons. God's invitation is to come out. Knowing some restless, seeking woman, ill at ease with herself and with her world, I have often thought, *She needs to sit on the Lord's lap and let him love her and quiet her a bit.* I have sat there often myself and come away refreshed in my own person. It's the Lord's promise, you know. "As one whom her mother comforts, so I will comfort you."[1]

---

[1] Isaiah 66:13

2

The Side Issue

Adam was probably the first Freudian who traced his problem to sexuality. He looked at the state he was in and complained to God about the woman God had given him. Men and women have been blaming each other for their troubles ever since. But sexuality is God's idea, and for all the flurry over the male-female controversy, no one can imagine life without it.

Sexuality is not synonymous with *sex,* as this word is used today. The sexual aspect of life unfortunately is often reduced to the sex act, something almost apart from our persons. Sexuality is far more encompassing, and our failure to understand this impoverishes us. We are sexual beings. The very fact of your human existence means that you are a sexual being. Sexuality is part of the divine creative order; it is personality incarnate as male or female.

That's obvious, you say. But I would go beyond that to say obviously good. Not just a fact, but a positive contribution to life. Sexuality is not tacked on to selfhood but belongs to its essence. Sexuality is the way I express who I am to others. In that sense, everything I do is sexual because I am a woman. To be a woman is a total way of existing.

God made the man, placed him in a garden and invited

him to participate creatively with the Godhead. Man was given the privilege of naming all the creatures God had created. It was serious business. For the Bible says that whatever Adam called the animals that was their name. That kind of partnership in creativity never fails to excite me. Imagine the thrill of Adam's task.

But, the Genesis account continues, Adam found no one of his kind in all creation. He was alone. God knows the joy of unity because he experiences this wholeness within the trinity to an extent that we cannot understand. In fact *oneness* is God's idea; it is a God concept. Knowing the joy of completion, of oneness, of fellowship God declared that it was not good for man to be alone.

So God fashioned someone like the man in kind, yet different in function. A person to complement and complete Adam. He recognized immediately that this was "bone of my bone and flesh of my flesh." He called her *woman* because she was taken out of man, and he received her joyfully. Then follows a most important and beautiful verse defining marriage, a verse quoted by Jesus and Paul in the New Testament, *Therefore, a man leaves his father and his mother and cleaves to his wife, and they become one flesh.* (Genesis 2:24)

Humanity is both male and female, not one or the other. Genesis 1:27 reads, *So God created man in his own image, in the image of God he created him: male and female he created them.* It is important to note that only when both male and female are created does the text speak of their being made in the image of God. A unity. Mankind, as opposed to animal-kind. Together male and female represent man made in the image of God. Together they are given dominion over the earth.

The generic term *man* includes woman. The word *Adam* also means mankind, as in Genesis 5:2, *Male and female he created them, and he blessed them and named them Man (or Adam) when they were created.* The creation account clearly and profoundly links male and female into a unity. Far more than being a "helper," woman is essential to man's being. Priority of creation *may* indicate male headship, but there is no evidence of superiority. The two are side by side in creation.

We often think in terms of masculine and feminine characteristics. Both are found within the personality of God. God is both male and female in that sense. He is mother and father. Male alone was incomplete. A fuller representation of God's image necessitated female. Man and woman together represent the image of God.

Therefore, I believe it is superficial to say that the difference between the male and the female is merely physiological. If that were the only difference, it would still not be so "mere," since a woman's physiology permeates and conditions her daily life more directly than a man's does. In fact, it is one of the burdens many women resent. One thing seems obvious; woman is not a man with feminine features anymore than a man is a woman with masculine features. A common humanness exists, which includes mental and spiritual equality, but God had more in mind than procreation when he made male and female.

Woman is a separate creative act of God. She is like the man and yet different. She has proven herself to be the equal of man, but that is different than being equal *to* or the same. We err if we over-emphasize sameness, and we fall into a trap of another kind if we specialize only in differences. Suffice it to say here that woman brings different gifts to the world, and this observation placed into experience has been the joy and conflict of many lives.

I labor over this because some of the currents of thought today begrudge the idea that God should be spoken of as a male. Some even object that the term *mankind* is prejudiced against women. God is Spirit. He is represented to us in ways which we can understand, and thus he is spoken of as God, the Father. Personally I find the Fatherhood of God a vastly comforting experience, and it seems to me that all that is implied in his fatherhood is found at the core of the universe.

If we are personally diminished by the male reference to God, we have not begun in any way to come to terms with our own sexuality. God made me a woman, and although all the world were to be male-dominated and oppressive, I believe he expects me to carry my womanhood with dignity and honor because it is not inferior in his sight.

The divine design is no mistake. The mutual attraction of male and female calls us out of our aloneness, out of our independence to see that we need each other. It is the foundation of human history. We are meant to enhance each other, to affirm the other's personhood and to discover that in our mutual dependence we solve the mystery of our existence.

Obviously, something has gone awry in the relationship between men and women. The unity, the complementing, the enhancing has become the rare experience, rather than the normal. Absorption with sex as a commodity or an experience has dehumanized both men and women so that an act becomes more important than personhood. Sex clouds our appreciation of sexuality. Sexuality belongs to the essence of our person, and if this were properly understood we could be content with an emphasis on accepting ourselves as persons.

Perhaps because I am a woman I believe that women suffered the greatest loss as the result of the Fall. I have speculated on Satan's strategy in making his approach through the woman. (An interesting sidetrack: I have never heard any objections to the male-ness of Satan!) Was there something inherent in her nature that made her more receptive to his deceit? (And was there likewise a receptivity to his wife that influenced Adama's behavior?) Whatever the answer, a disaster took place. Both the man and woman hid themselves from the presence of God. This simple sentence — both tragic and profound — is the key to understanding subsequent history.

Everything changed for both the man and the woman. Henceforth the man would toil to obtain his food all the days of his life, the very ground of the earth working against him. Thorns, thistles, the sweat of his face. Sin's disorder more directly affected the woman's person. Childbirth would be painful; her own body would work against her. Her desire would be for her husband and her husband would rule over her. Sin was let loose in the world. Selfishness. One-up-manship. Exploitation. Domination. Fatigue. Unrest. Abuse. Deceit. The misery of meeting self's needs. The loss of identity.

Conceit and moral perversion led men away from God's ideal in the mutual creation of mankind. Men began to see women as inferior and for their own use. The farther men went from the divine revelation, the darker the picture for women. Her loss of prestige and her rightful place besides man degenerated steadily, and history indicates that the darkest years came after 1000 b.c. One of the first indications of this decline in the Bible is found when Lamech took two wives. Polygamy was never sanctioned by God and directly opposes the principle found in Genesis 2:24. God receives considerable blame from contemporary feminists for the subjection of women. Blaming God for mankind's troubles is consistent with our perverse nature; the subjection of women was born out of sinfulness.

A study of history reveals that the ancient Hebrews, in contrast to the pagan nations around them, never completely lost the ideal God had given them at creation. In the law, for instance, children were instructed to honor both father and mother. Many women of excellent spirit rose to prominence and national leadership in Israel. Women were judges, poets and leaders. One thinks of Miriam, Deborah, Huldah, Hannah, and others. Even the power of a wicked Jezebel shows the extent of women's influence in Israel. History records that Queen Alexandra during the inter-testamental period initiated compulsory education for both boys and girls, a revolutionary concept at that time, thus banishing illiteracy in Palestine. Yet the Old Testament also records discrimination against women, the adoption of pagan practices, and the prophets' outcry against the desecration of marriage (Malachi 2). The Bible is very honest in recording wickedness.

The desire to dominate, to subjugate another, to be superior comes out of the heart of mankind set in opposition to God. We have only to think of galley slaves in Mediterranean ships to realize that women have not been the only ones to suffer. In fact, wherever women have been able to maneuver the situation, they have dominated men with a variety of weapons, leaving their own mark on history. But when a Jew prayed, "I thank thee that I am not a woman," he was not reflecting the viewpoint of God anymore than the contemporary church does when it expresses prejudice. It seems natural for mankind to try to find someone to look down upon. And others take pride in "looking down on those who look down on people."

Even at the height of their culture, a low view of women existed in the Greek and Roman worlds. Noble women are mentioned, as well as business women like Lydia, but only in Greek art and poetry are women heroines. Aristotle is said to have taught that women were inferior in every way, only a rank above slaves. Xenophon, the historian, recorded these prejudices and wrote that women are best kept confined to an "inside world." Plato advocated community wives. Goddesses, fertility rites, and prostitution in pagan temples scarred the lives of both the men and women to whom Paul preached in Gentile cities. In the city of Corinth, for instance, a thousand prostitutes were kept in the temple as part of pagan worship. Without question the life of the early church was complicated by the experience of the people in it and this is the context of Paul's teaching about women and the problems of marriage. First Corinthians 7 must be read in light of the entangled relationships which must have existed in a new church born out of such a culture.

But light comes to the darkness. God comes incarnate in Jesus Christ to restore mankind to himself. The Son of God confines himself to a woman's womb and is dependent on her care and nurture. That one event alone restored women's status. Mary's song is a song of enoblement by God. As Jesus becomes a grown man he moves about in the company of women with a freedom unknown to the teachers of his day. Even his disciples marveled that he, a teacher, should hold a conversation with a woman in public. And to that very woman (see John 4) he gave the first revelation that he was the Messiah. He was direct and natural in his manner with women, never stooping to a patronizing or domineering role.

Jesus regularly taught women the Scriptures, a practice

not normally allowed in Judaism. He commended Mary for taking the "male role" in sitting at his feet and listening to his teaching. He refused to force her into a typical stereotype when he told Martha that Mary had chosen that better part. In fact, he treated both of them as persons who could exercise their own priorities.

In Jewish tradition a woman was not permitted to bear witness. Jesus deliberately broke that tradition and commissioned women to be the first witnesses of the resurrection. He said, "Go, tell the disciples . . ." He also broke the taboo about the ritual uncleanness of a menstrous woman by curing the woman who had an issue of blood for twelve years. He did not simply cure her quietly, but called public attention to the fact that she had touched him, and he did not shrink from her touch.

When a woman called out, "Blessed is the womb that bore you and the breasts that you sucked!" Jesus rejected that limited view of women and affirmed a greater view of personhood by replying, "Blessed rather are those who hear the word of God and keep it!"

A careful reading of the gospels reveals that Jesus sought to give equal dignity to women in many ways. When he wanted to illustrate how much God loves lost people, he told three parables. In the first, the shepherd, who leaves ninety-nine sheep to seek the lost one, represents God. In the second parable, a woman seeking a lost coin represents God. In the third, a father longs for this son, and the father is God.

Unquestionably Jesus made a sharp break with contemporary culture by giving women full dignity and freedom as persons. Women were not only the first to believe, but were honored with some of the most significant revelations about Jesus. He is Christ, the Liberator, restoring us to God and offering to redeem our prejudices, our failures, and our position in life.

Because of him Paul could write, *There is neither Jew nor Greek, there is neither slave nor free, there is neither male nor female; for you are all one in Christ Jesus.*

Years have passed since his coming. The patterns of sin are deeply ingrained in our society. The abuses of the past have left many women with a loss of personhood, of self-value. Bible verses quoted out of context to prove that woman's existence is for man continue to validate a kind of servitude in some circles. It is appalling to think that as late as the early 1900's women were treated as second class citizens, without the right to vote, to hold property or to go to court. If a girl did not marry, few careers were open to her. Time has erased many of the prohibitions of the past, and yet today women are crusading for equal pay for equal jobs and for the opportunity to enter certain professions. Many university women especially feel discriminated against and have responded with an anger that amounts to man-hatred.

The church, often too conservative and slow to move, reads the magnificent tribute of a king to his mother in Proverbs 31 on Mother's Day, and over-estimates the transcultural significance of Paul's instructions for women to keep silent the rest of the year. They forget about Philip's four daughters who prophesied and about Priscilla, who was a co-worker with Paul, who taught Apollos and whose name is often mentioned before that of her husband in the work of the church.

That's the background of the world in which we live. Meanwhile, women have not always been examples of godliness in the face of this stress. Their strengths and their gifts have been twisted out of shape. The instructions of the New Testament that irritate women today were necessitated by real life situations, interestingly as real today as the day they were written. *Women should not be slanderers, but temperate, faithful in all things. Young widows who grow wanton against Christ in their desire to marry. Idlers, gossips, busybodies, saying what they should not.* Paul was helping churches in a pagan world to see that those who believed in Jesus were to have conduct worthy of the Gospel. And one of the things that most impressed the first century world was the honor and chastity within the Christian home and the integrity of interpersonal relationships. The pagan Libanius is said to have exclaimed, "What women these Christians are!" That same witness is needed today.

Suffering from exploitation, women have found ways to exploit others: manipulation, playing the distorted female image for all it is worth. Accepting your sexuality precludes this kind of behavior. Men alone have not made women sex-objects; women have let them do it. While seeming to resist, they respond to all the clamor of sexual come-on by the products they buy and the way they act. I've watched girls with good minds and high ambitions stoop to the silliest of maneuvers, turning their backs on their best friends, to gain what they thought was that experience of supreme value — the attention of a male.

At the other end of the spectrum are the scared ones who can endure no healthy, wholesome friendships with men. They cut themselves off into exclusive friendships with their own sex, and repudiating the natural attraction between men and women, they grow prudish and are types of atrophied humanity.

Neither of these have accepted their sexuality and found fulfillment in their personhood. A healthy freedom shines out from the one who can celebrate the joy of being a woman. Shout it out. This chaotic, tension-filled, sex-oriented world has plenty of room for a free and joyous acceptance of womanhood. Redeemed womanhood has a kind of clear, wholesome atmosphere about it that has an uplifting effect on everyone.

A person's attitude toward her sexuality manifests itself in all of her behavior: the way she finds fulfillment, her acceptance of responsibility, her self-discipline, her ability to give herself in relationships, her attitude toward men and her treatment of other women. The woman struggling with self-acceptance rarely likes other women. She may use them for her purposes, but her loyalty is thin even toward those who seem closest to her. She may avoid women completely and opt to radiate in the presence of men, and thus fulfill a need for approval and identity, but she is wary of relationships which demand anything of her.

Learning integrity in one's emotional life is never easy, especially in the face of our present culture, so plastic and pervaded with dishonesty. Yet I feel it must be learned

if a woman is to experience the fulfillment and commitment of meaningful relationships.

What do I mean by this? Simply wholeness. Putting it
together so that your personhood and your sexuality are in
harmony. You've accepted yourself. You have stopped
grabbing at life to fill your own needs. You face reality
honestly. You can relax and be wholesomely you — not
celebrating your hang-ups, but celebrating the joyful acceptance of being a woman and the freedom to give yourself in your relationships.

The potential for this kind of wholeness is made possible
by the redemption found in Jesus Christ. The answer to
accepting your sexuality is the same as the answer to accepting yourself. Jesus Christ has redeemed us; He will
redeem our personalities, our relationships, our expression
of self in the world. He tells us who we are and what we
can do. He puts our priorities straight; he fills our empty
spots so that we are kept from seeking fulfillment in the
wrong places. He understands women. He understands
you.

Then why, you ask, does the Bible give all these sticky
statements about women being silent, treating them as if
they can't think or aren't real people? I believe Paul's
statements are in a cultural setting and that his words have
been blown out of proportion. Let's take a look at some
of the thornier passages.

The passages in question come from two sources: the
letter to the Corinthians and Paul's letter to Timothy at
Ephesus. Both letters are written in the context of the
Greco-Roman culture where women were discriminated
against and given inferior status. Temple prostitution was
part of life. Small wonder that converted women hardly
knew how to act when they were included in the church.
First Corinthians 14:34-35 tells women to keep silent in
the church and to be subordinate even as the law says.
If women had questions they were to ask their husbands
at home. But the verse which immediately precedes this
reads, "For God is not a God of confusion, but of peace."

The last half of the Corinthian letter answers questions
posed to Paul (1 Corinthians 7:1) by the church. We

don't know specifically what the questions were, but clearly the Corinthian church was having troubles. Its members were people redeemed from a life of passion and intemperance. They needed to be taught how to partake of the Lord's supper without getting drunk or being gluttons (1 Corinthians 11) and how to use spiritual gifts without excess (1 Corinthians 12-14.) It is interesting to note that the instructions about women are in the context of the teaching about tongue-speaking. Perhaps women were the greatest abusers of this gift and caused disruption in the church. Or perhaps they haggled over the interpretation of tongues. Whatever, their public fuss reflected poorly on their husbands and on the church in the sight of unbelievers.

Obviously women did pray and prophesy in the church because First Corinthians 11:5-6 gives instructions about the way it should be done. In the culture of that day it was only modest and appropriate for a woman to pray with her head covered, thus showing reverence to God and to her husband. In the same chapter Paul goes back to the creation ideal to instruct these Gentiles about the interdependence of the man and woman, made in the image of God (vs. 8-12). It seems entirely possible that a repressed group of women were experiencing new acceptance and freedom in Christ that was almost too much to handle. The weakness of the average man in spiritual leadership could be the real source of these instructions. God has charged men with leadership and perhaps too many of them were being threatened and not assuming their responsibility.

Perhaps the most difficult passage is found in Paul's first letter to Timothy, chapter 2:8-15. Again Timothy is being told how to instruct a Gentile church in Ephesus, where the goddess Artemis was worshiped. Men are to learn to pray without anger or quarreling. Women are to be modest in apparel and full of good deeds. Then comes the cruncher: *Let a woman learn in silence with all submissiveness. I permit no woman to have authority over men; she is to keep silent. For Adam was formed first, then Eve; and Adam was not deceived, but the woman was deceived and became a transgressor. Yet woman will be saved through bearing children, if she continues in faith and love and holiness, with modesty.*

At first glance the last sentence of the quotation seems to teach works-righteousness, rather than salvation by faith. Nowhere in Scripture is salvation conditioned by our good works, let alone child-bearing, which in some circumstances would hardly qualify as a good work! The Greek word commonly translated in this passage *saved* can as appropriately be translated *vindicated*. New Testament scholar Dr. William Lane suggests that a preferred translation would read, "Yet woman will be vindicated by the birth of the Child . . ." This rendition recognizes the allusion to Genesis 3:15 in the passage, which follows naturally on the reference to Eve in verse 13. It appears to be consistent with the full teaching of Scripture; it eliminates controversial questions about salvation; it underscores the relationship of this sentence to Paul's larger argument.

But we are still left with the statement about the silence of women. Notice how translators have handled the Greek text of verse 12.

> But I suffer not a woman to teach nor to usurp authority over the man, but to be in silence. (KJV)

> Personally I don't allow women to teach, nor do I even put them in positions of authority over men — I believe their role is to be receptive. (Phillips paraphrase.)

> I do not permit a woman to be a teacher, nor must woman domineer over man; she should be quiet. (NEB)

> I do not permit a married woman to practice teaching or domineering over a husband; she must keep quiet. (Williams)

A strong case can be made that this is Paul's way of handling a difficult problem, perhaps one which challenged the spiritual authority of young Timothy. The issue seems to be the usurping of authority by women. There may well have been in Ephesus a woman responsible for the doctrinal chaos in the church (1 Timothy 1:3-7). This was certainly true of another Asian church less than a generation later (Revelation 2:20).

We have no difficulty in making cultural adjustments for instructions about meat offered to idols or the injunction to greet one another with a holy kiss or other such instructions in both letters — because the weight of Scripture does not bear out their transcultural importance. The rules of biblical interpretation require us to give the passage the obvious meaning intended by the author in the context in which he wrote and to allow Scripture to interpret Scripture. I submit that in the teaching about silence Paul is addressing a specific problem in a specific place.

However, what is the principle behind both the problem and the instruction? It is that God has charged men with spiritual leadership. Paul uses curious reasoning. He observes that Eve was deceived, but do we observe in addition that Adam knew what he was doing? That would seem to make him as guilty, if not more so, as the woman. He too is a transgressor. The temptation of Adam came through the person to whom he was most vulnerable — his own wife. Only those who know the power of *one flesh* can grasp both the tenderness and tragedy of what happened at the Fall. Eve was part of him — his very own flesh. The man and the woman were an entity, knowing only perfect trust and mutuality. The master tempter knew Eve's point of vulnerability as well as Adam's; he exploited her natural emotional concerns for her family unit. Thus did sin enter the world. Ever since the Fall husbands have been given the responsibility of spiritual leadership, which is not a light burden to bear. God holds them responsible.

The principle of the male leadership is found throughout Scripture and cannot be explained away on cultural terms. Similarly the principle of modesty for women seems to be consistent in the Bible and would preclude usurping authority or disrupting the church. To speak of equal standing before God is to talk of a different matter for both men and women. Peter makes a point of this when he speaks of the husband and the wife as "heirs together of the grace of life."

I submit that the early church fathers were more strongly influenced by Aristotle and Xenophon, the major voices in Greek culture, than they were by the total teaching of Scripture. Paul is unjustly blamed for what has happened in history. In fact, Paul's accounts of the role of women in the early church are astounding in light of the place of women in the culture in which he worked. But Scripture has not been read without cultural prejudice. One can hardly conceive that the church fathers could write as they did on this subject if they understood the significance and magnificence of Paul's instruction that a man love his wife as Christ loved the church!

Instead Tertullian spoke of women as "the mother of all ills." Chrysostom wrote of women as "a natural temptation and desirable calamity, a deadly fascination," almost as if woman were designed by Satan instead of created in the image of God. Thomas Aquinas betrayed his prejudice by agreeing with Aristotle that "woman is a misbegotten male," a statement that hardly honors God's creation. St. Augustine agreed with the Greco-Roman tradition that a woman's sole function was procreation. In fact, I find the writings of the early church fathers on this subject appalling! And we are still saddled today with remnants of this male interpretation of theology.

A similar study could be made on the cultural attitude to slavery. Paul told Onesimus, a newly converted runaway slave, to return to his owner, but by doing this he did not condone slavery. Think how many years it has taken for society, with a growing Christian influence, to break the chains of slavery. Yet Paul had written earlier to Galatian Christians that Christ had come to break down all these man-made barriers: Jew — Gentile, Slave — Free; Male — Female. He told Ephesian Christians that God is without partiality.

Prejudice is passed on from generation to generation in insidious ways. Thus it is difficult to stand back and make honest and careful evaluations. If we admit to these two scriptural principles, we must ask some hard questions. What is spiritual leadership, and what is repressive, egotistical domination? Is spiritual leadership merely serving as an elder in the church? What kind of leadership represents Christ's care for the church? And what is modesty? We have been gloriously inconsistent. Is modesty outward fashion, mindless silence, or a heart that responds to God (and thus to her husband) with godly tenderness?

The idea that women should not teach and always be silent is contradicted by the example of Philip's daughters, by Priscilla who taught Apollos, and by the large number of women mentioned in Romans 16 who were active in spreading the Christian message. Philippians 4:3 mentions two women who "labored side by side with me in the gospel." Furthermore, many women have exceptional gifts of teaching and administration, as well as high intelligence. Did God give these in vain? That we made a rigid rule out of a cultural problem seems a blight on the freedom which Christ himself afforded women and the personal encouragement he gave them. I believe the weight of biblical emphasis gives godly women more freedom than has yet been realized. The problem is godliness and the godly exercise of gifts by both men and women.

I reaffirm that women are not captive to an ancient cultural problem. But we do need to consider what is special about the gifts God has given women when he completed mankind. Probably nothing raises the hackles of women who feel boxed in by categories more than mentioning differences. While wanting to avoid stereotypes I think an appreciation of ourselves demands that we deal realistically with differences and gifts.

For instance, by design the function of the male requires that he be assertive. The function of the woman necessitates that she be a willing recipient. In that sense, I suppose we could say biology is destiny. But I am not a humanist; biology is not accidental. It is interesting to observe that the Hebrew word for man, *ish*, means strong. The word for woman *ishshah* means soft and delicate. These are matter-of-fact observations and their implications help us understand manifestations of sexuality. The danger is in making rigid categories so that a woman is never an initiator, a man is never tender, and a woman comes out of the cookie-cutter as passive and weak, and the man is domineering and superior.

A person can be many things at once. To say that one thing is true about any person is not to say that some other trait is not sometimes also present. A given trait does not make one inferior nor superior. Neither, I submit, do we define personal worth by the kind of job an individual does. And any woman who has come to terms with her sexuality certainly does not use the criteria of her attractiveness to men as a measure of her value.

The question is often raised, whether men and women are really so different after all, apart from biological differences. The proponents of equality call attention to men who are cooks, tailors or teachers and women who are lawyers, doctors or business women. Nothing is proved by this except that both sexes are capable of performing a variety of kinds of work and doing so with equal intelligence. But studies also indicate that given the same situation and the same position women will react differently than men. Quite apart from the studies and controversies over this, my own observation says this is so.

I think of a couple working together on a project who were attempting to decide how many people would attend a given seminar. The man gathered statistics and plotted out a graph to arrive at his conclusions. The woman took various human factors into account and intuitively decided that a given number would attend. Both arrived at the same number — which was precisely the number which came. This is not to say that a woman might never plot out a graph. It is simply an observation reinforced by experience. Nor, I emphasize, is it to comment on which way of reaching a conclusion is best.

At the risk of being misunderstood by the equalitarians, I join those who assert that a different pulse beats in the veins of a woman. Emotionally they look at the world differently. I believe God has given the woman special sensitivities and gifts — and responsibilities — in the emotional realm which enhance mankind. She has a special sensitivity to the needs of others, which includes an almost intuitive understanding of situations and people's feelings.

Her empathy makes it natural for her to feel the hurts of others. She has a highly developed capacity for love and for giving of herself. Attention to detail is a natural gift, especially important because she has the creative ability to bear children and is responsible for their care. She introduces color, harmony, joy, light-heartedness into human life. Berdysen remarks that woman is the doorway into community. Others have declared that women have a civilizing effect on the world because of their natural gifts.

Ah, you say, I know men who are sensitive to others, too. So do I. And I know women who are not. That does not invalidate the generality. Nor do I think of these as rigid categories that confine women. I believe they enhance her self-appreciation. They need to be emphasized because we are losing what the world needs in our strain to be equal. Equality is not what women need, but the right to develop to our fullest potential to be what God wants us to be. And the last phrase of that sentence is important. The job we do is relatively unimportant; what we *are* is critical.

Commenting on the difference in the sexes says nothing about intelligence or ability to think — or inherent value in spiritual terms. I am not complimented when I am told that I think like a man or drive like a man. For me a man is not the standard. I am a woman. The best of femaleness is the standard.

But we strain too much on this point. Once we've accepted femininity we can get on with being a person — a feminine person. *Feminine* defined is simply that pertaining to being a woman. It's not the ruffles we wear, it's the person God made us. And expressions of femininity will vary with our genes and ambitions, but they will be feminine because that is what we are. Feminine can mean continuing to grow, tapping the potential of our minds and hearts as well as our wombs. It can mean rejoicing in the force of life within us and being present in every moment in all that we do.

Do not let others poison your joy in being created female. The possibilities inherent in being made woman are as creative as the God who made us. And there is great dignity in his design.

3

One Step from Eden

Doing your own thing is "in" these days. It's especially in for women, who more recently have been revealed to be supposedly the largest oppressed group in the world. Everyone needs to express themselves, to have a little elbow room to discover new dimensions of their personalities. Affluence allows it. The climate of permissiveness encourages it. A contagious fever rages. The voice of selfishness is heard in our land.

No, I can't really take a church school class. You see, I've got a season-pass at Summit Ski Lodge, and I go there every weekend I can. . . . Well, skiing really does do more for me than teaching wiggling sixth-graders on Sunday morning, don't you think? I find it more fulfilling.

Could my son be in your Cub Scout den? . . . No, I can't be a helper really. You see, I work. . . . Yes, I felt I wanted to use my training instead of letting it go to waste. And I just love it. The only problem with the job is that it takes me away some evenings. . . . No, she's only two, but I drop her off at a babysitter. . . . Why yes. Would store-bought cookies be all right?

The Old People's Home? Well, I'm no good with old people at all. I'm afraid I just couldn't. Besides I'm spending all my free time making a new wardrobe for my trip to Greece this summer. . . . Yeah, Marge and I are going. It's our third summer abroad. . . . Well, I really am sorry I don't have time to help.

I just couldn't take it any longer. After all, being confined with two pre-schoolers gets pretty dreary. You get so you just long for adult company. . . . Well, Tom helps me with the housework in the evenings, and it really works out quite well. . . . Sounds interesting, but I don't have time to read. I hardly ever find time even to read to the kids.

Well, the weeks go by fast. On Monday nights I wash my clothes, on Tuesdays I wash my hair. Wednesdays I usually go home and have dinner with my parents so I don't have to cook a big meal. Thursdays I clean the apartment and on Fridays I go home again. I usually sleep in on Saturdays and then go shopping for clothes with my mother or my aunt.

No thanks. We just enjoy being by ourselves. We don't like the inconvenience of having to entertain others back. We usually spend the early evenings watching television, then have a glass of milk and go to bed. It's peaceful and quiet with just us two.

I watch our kids being neglected, and I can't do anything about it. I want to finish my degree and she's determined to finish hers. She asks what right I have to do it if she can't. Actually, we're very competitive. She won't give in and let me be first, and I won't give in and let her be first. It's kind of a stalemate in leadership, and our children suffer for it.

Conversations like these are as varied as the people speaking. *And none of them are really wrong, morally I mean. Couldn't good motivation prompt their point of view, factors we don't know about? I mean, after all, it's their decision.*

But we are also "deciders," and we need to ask ourselves if there is something eccentric[1] in today's freedom to do your own thing.

Responsibility has become almost a dirty word. A bit Puritan and repressive. Freedom and responsibility seem to oppose each other. Hardly anyone asks, Am I free enough to be responsible?

---

[1] eccentric: off center

Significantly the Bible says little about rights, but much about responsibility. Freedom is a dominant theme, but it is the freedom offered by Jesus Christ — freedom from sin, from self and from unworthy choices. In fact, a potent warning says, "You were called to freedom; only do not use your freedom as an opportunity for the flesh, but through love be servants of one another" (Galatians 5:13). That's biblical freedom — freedom to love and serve someone else.

Freedom is a staggering concept — easier to talk about than to experience. Its counterfeits are many. How many enticements to freedom have led people into a grim kind of slavery rather than into the adventure they sought! Genuine freedom is the great adventure, because it links us up with God who is prime Innovator and Creator. It is quite different from doing "your own thing."

Personal freedom demands that we choose the quality of our adventure. In fact, we must decide what our adventure will be. We cannot give ourselves to two adventures at the same time. We must decide what is worthwhile. Too many people live with divided hearts and their lives are fragmented with a little bit of this and a little bit of that. None of it fits into a meaningful pattern and the person, having made no decision and no commitment to what is worthwhile, wastes years — or a lifetime. An ironic tragedy is to aim at nothing and to hit it. Or perhaps worse still, to aim at the wrong thing and hit it.

I have sometimes thought that I'd like to be a dozen different people. One of me could be an interior decorator and I could spend someone else's money as an exciting outlet for some flambouyant ideas I'd like to try out. I'd like to be a professor. I'd like to be a foreign correspondent or teach overseas. Whenever I go into a restaurant that has the extra touch of charm, I think it would be fun to run a cozy place that is not run-of-the-mill.

I'd like to be a partner in a business with my husband because I think he is clever and I would have fun being his first assistant. I'd like to write a column for a newspaper. I'd like to sail around the world in our own sailboat. You name it. I'd probably think it would be fun to try. But alas, I am only one person. And with my one life I must determine the most valuable way to spend it in the will of God.

Deciding on what is worthwhile demands having a standard, a measure outside ourselves. On what basis will you judge what is worthwhile? The principle of pleasure has proved an unreliable guide. "But I enjoy doing this" hardly passes as a statement of value. The principle of success has seen more than its share of catastrophes. Paul Tournier says, "Every one of us feels that there is a hierarchy of choices, that a person can succeed in many things without believing his life worthwhile."

What is worthwhile must have meaning in an ultimate sense, in God's sight, so that all the small pieces of each day, though they be trivial, will fit in with that meaning. Existence is not absurd, as Camus would have us believe. It forms part of a coherent plan laid down by the Creator. Our personal choices or adventures are only significant as they are in harmony with the adventure or plan of God.

Furthermore, every choice of what is worthwhile necessitates that we reject some other good possibilities. Robert Frost[2] reminds us of that.

> Two roads diverged in a yellow wood,
> And sorry I could not travel both
> And be one traveler, long I stood
> And looked down one as far as I could
> To where it bent in the undergrowth. . . .
>
> I shall be telling this with a sigh
> Somewhere ages and ages hence:
> Two roads diverged in a wood, and I —
> I took the one less traveled by,
> And that has made all the difference.

What is good is not necessarily worthwhile for me. *Good* can crowd out *best*. A profession, a mate, a course of study seem to be critical roads to us. But the same principle ap-

---

[2] From "The Road Not Taken" from *The Poetry of Robert Frost* edited by Edward Connery Lathem. Copyright 1916, © 1969 Holt, Rinehart and Winston, Inc. Copyright 1944 by Robert Frost. Reprinted by permission of Holt, Rinehart and Winston.

plies to the small choices in life. They must fit into a larger picture.

Skiing is a good thing. That I go every weekend may not be worthwhile. Intellectual interests outside the home are commendable, but if they cause neglect of the people I love most, then they are not worthwhile. With mobility and affluence, I'm convinced that some people live at such a fast and hectic pace that they have never discovered life's other possibilities. Possibilities like peace and quiet for meditation, family sharing, and listening to God. The question is one of long range goals which fit into the will of God, of thinking beyond our present experience so that life is not haphazard, but meaningful.

Contemporary woman has never had so many choices, but that has not assured that her life will be more worthwhile than when she was imprisoned to home and hearth. She may just be rushing to get the front seat on the bus without knowing where it is going. The outcome can resemble a woman let loose for the first time in a fashionable store; a bit of this and a little of that, but none of it fits together to make a costume. An orange floppy hat with pajamas! Like a small girl trying on her mother's clothes; it's only funny when you are little. Because when you grow up and make irresponsible choices it hurts others besides yourself.

Furthermore, we tend to ask such small questions about our role in life. For instance, students ask me, "Do you like housework?" I suppose they ask that because it represents the epitome of slavery to them, and because they seem unaware that any commitment has its less exciting moments. I never ask myself that question. It is irrelevant. It is akin to asking a student if she likes to study, or a man if he likes to drive to work. Housework is only a small part of a larger picture I am painting with my life. Does an artist like cleaning her brushes? I don't discuss the pleasure of housework; I do it. And yet questions like these often mark the small talk of women. Are we that confused?

Do I like housework? And who will be influenced by my life? These are two different kinds of questions. If I answer the latter, I may more gladly accept the former. Our problem is that we often do not even know when questions are not of the same value. Hence, we have difficulty fitting short range goals into long range satisfactions.

Discovering what is worthwhile changes our orientation to life. We can feel *called* or *appointed* to a role in life, instead of chafing at the bit or feeling used. Less consumed with being fulfilled, we are free to fulfill our calling. But this necessitates the kind of acceptance of personhood that we have been discussing. It requires real freedom.

The confusion and tragedy of the contemporary Women's Lib movement is that women are being led to think that children, housework, or the confines of marriage are the cause of their personal frustration when the root cause lies deeply within their own personhood. The diagnosis is wrong and the result is wasteful and destructive.

"The victim of this confidence game believes with all her heart that her only satisfactions are going to be those earned by leading an independent life, remaining loyal to abstractions, and doing her own thing. She cannot allow herself to believe that these misty ideals may actually be substitutes for the give-and-take of intensely personal relationships and extended personal commitments — where love is not something you go around talking about but something you do."[3]

On the other side of the fence stands the single woman who believes all her problems would be solved if she had the love of a good man, children, and a home in which to express her creative talents. She may be unaware that she longs for this man and these children, not to share with them the richness and satisfactions of her own life, but to make up for all that is empty inside her. She, as well, may reveal an incapacity to give of herself in interpersonal relationship.

Many of the illnesses people suffer express this kind of dissatisfaction with life. It is a cover-up for lack of commitment and the freedom to see beyond immediacy. No

---

[3] Anne Bernays, *Atlantic*, March, 1970, p. 107.

decision about what is valuable, what is meaningful, no commitment to God or to others is paralyzing.

Fulfillment is not so much trying something new as it is coming to terms with your present situation. God, who is creative, may add a splash of color here and a new experience there, but it will always line up with your responsibility to fulfill the commitment made.

A little boy once said to the housemother of his boarding school, "You are kind, but you do not love us." Not only little boys are perceptive about the loving ones. When someone is living for self, disinterested, limping along without commitment, she announces it to the whole world by her priorities and behavior. The common expression, "Her heart is not in it" comes to mind. When a person commits herself to what is really worthwhile, she becomes part of the flow of the love of God. And her heart is in it.

How do we get our hearts into it? We begin by going to God.

> ". . . Faith, far from turning us away from the world, brings us back to it. That is why it awakens in us a new interest in the world, in the concrete reality of every day, hard, laborious, difficult, often painful as it is, but wonderful nevertheless. The joy of living, of making an effort, of having a worthwhile goal to aim at; the joy of moving a finger . . . of looking at something, of hearing a voice, of learning something and loving someone."[4]

Loving others puts our hearts back into the stream of life. It is worthwhile and valuable. It is full of fresh surprises and new discoveries. Loving is our responsibility. We have the example of God who commits Himself, who is not passive in His responsibility but charges Himself with our personal care. This kind of godliness on our part marks our fulfillment. It gives us enthusiasm (the feeling of God inside us) for living. It changes the mundane, the trivial, so that in all circumstances of life goodness reaches out to others.

If this is your thing, do it with all your might.

---

[4] Paul Tournier, *The Adventure of Living* (p. 236), reprinted by permission from Harper & Row, Inc.

4

The Liberated Woman

Crying is all right in its way while it lasts. But you have to stop sooner or later and then you still have to decide what to do. When Jill stopped, she found she was dreadfully thirsty. She had been lying face downward, and now she sat up . . . she listened carefully and felt almost sure what she heard was the sound of running water.

The woods was so still that it was not difficult to decide where the sound was coming from. . . . Sooner than she expected she came to an open glade and saw the stream, bright as glass, running across the turf a stone's throw away from her. But although the sight of the water made her feel ten times thirstier than before, she didn't rush forward and drink. She stood as still as if she had been turned into stone, with her mouth open. And she had a very good reason: just on this side of the stream lay the lion. . . .

"If you're thirsty, you may drink," . . .

For a second she stared here and there, wondering who had spoken. Then the voice said again, "If you are thirsty, come and drink . . ." it was the lion speaking. The voice was not like a man's. It was deeper, wilder and stronger; a sort of heavy, golden voice. It did not make her any less

frightened than she had been before, but it made her
frightened in rather a different way.

"Are you not thirsty?" said the Lion.

"I'm dying of thirst," said Jill.

"Then drink," said the Lion.

"May I — could I — would you mind going away while
I do," said Jill.

The Lion answered this only by a look and a very low
growl. . . .

The delicious rippling noise of the stream was driving
her nearly frantic.

"Will you promise not to — do anything to me, if I do
come?" said Jill.

"I make no promise," said the Lion.

Jill was so thirsty now that, without noticing it, she had
come a step nearer.

"Do you eat girls?" she said.

"I have swallowed up girls and boys, women and men,
kings and emperors, cities and realms," said the Lion. It
didn't say this as if it were boasting, nor as if it were sorry,
nor as if it were angry. It just said it.

"I daren't come and drink," said Jill.

"Then you will die of thirst," said the Lion.

"Oh dear!" said Jill, coming another step nearer. "I suppose I must go and look for another stream then."

"There is no other stream," said the Lion. . . .

It was the worst thing she had ever had to do, but she
went forward to the stream, knelt down, and began scoop-
ing up water in her hand. It was the coldest, most refreshing water she had ever tasted. You didn't need to drink
much of it, for it quenched your thirst at once. . . .

"Come here," said the Lion. And she had to.[1]

Thus C. S. Lewis tells his allegory of the liberation of
Jill in his book *The Silver Chair*.

That's the first step in liberation for any woman — meeting the Lion, quenching your thirst and feeling suddenly
safe. You may try other streams, but there are none. And

---

[1] Reprinted with permission of The Macmillan Company from
The Silver Chair by C. S. Lewis, copyright 1953 by The Macmillan Company.

you drink at his invitation. Jesus' invitation is, "If any one thirst, let him come to me and drink. He who believes in me . . . out of his heart shall flow rivers of living water."

All true liberation begins this way. What a person believes about God is the most important thing about her. If she insists on filling her own needs and depending on her own resources, she is shut up to the smallness of herself. On the other hand, when she comes to God, lets him be Lord in her life and trusts him to act on her behalf all his resources are at her disposal. And out of her own heart flow rivers of living water.

An encounter with God and entering into a personal relationship is not the same as being religious. Passionately religious women may still not know God. Emotionally they experience lofty thoughts that make them feel good; ideas about God stimulate them and they affirm their belief in him. Something is missing. The will. The total person has never submitted to the eternal, holy God. A personal encounter. A commitment which is irrevocable and life-changing — this is spiritual liberation.

When that happens, a woman has a basis on which to build her concerns about her place in the world. She knows *whose* she is and proceeds to find out *who* she is as a unique person. As she does so, she is increasingly liberated in social and personal ways. No two women will have exactly the same experiences, but given the control of the Holy Spirit within her, I suggest that a liberated woman's growing freedom will manifest itself in several of the following ways.

A liberated woman will not tie herself in psychic knots trying to prove she is not inferior. She experiences little anguish over the fact that there are no important women composers, and simply concludes that male brains operate best in composing as in some other areas. She rejoices that female brains can write poetry and novels and think of other beautiful things to add to the world.

She is not intimidated by the difference between men and women because difference doesn't mean inferior to her. She can see that women are as valuable as men, just as eyes and ears are both valuable, but not the same. Emotionally, biologically, and constitutionally she admits to differences without a hassle.

Frankly, she likes who she is and, amidst all the rhetoric, simply goes on being who she is with a sense of well-being about it. Some would say she is enslaved, but doesn't know it. Never mind. She's happier than her accusers.

Further, she will not waste her creative energy in rebellion against her lot in life, whether that be especially privileged or underprivileged. Because she believes in responsibility she does not leave for greener pastures on the other side of the fence. She exercises her womanhood creatively for the good of others and her own enrichment. She knows what she has been liberated for.

My mind scans the variety of experiences women have endured over the years, as I write this, and I shudder at some of them. The humiliating rape, the physical abuse. The women who have borne ten children with four miscarriages in fifteen years, only to be deserted, as was Mrs. Charles Dickens. The confinement, the lack of opportunity. The hard work. Yet triumph does not always come with banners and parade music. Often it is born quietly within the heart of a woman who will not let her circumstances destroy her person, and so my previous paragraph stands unedited.

No male injustice diminishes her value in her own eyes, nor does she allow it in the eyes of others. If a man cannot take a good suggestion from a woman lest it belittle him, she knows that says more about him than it does about her. (I have heard of men who will not even take help in finding a parking spot.) In fact, some men have later taken her good ideas, without recognition of their source, and made them their own. Never mind, she says, they need liberation, too. She has good-humoredly been the "token" woman on more than one committee, but she silences domineering men with a quality of life. She likes men as her counterpart in the creative order.

If someone were to ask her, "Are you most conscious of being a person or a woman?" she would affirm her personhood. Healthy women are conscious of being persons, as men are. They are persons who are women, not women trying to find personhood. It seems accurate to say that men make women most conscious of their womanhood, and I suppose the reverse is true as well. But an unhealthy woman is one who has no sense of self except as she exists in the eyes of men.

A liberated woman is not afraid of leadership. She does not hide her intellect, her ideas, or her abilities by feigning humility. If she is liberated, she has come to terms with herself. She can be who she is, with sensitivity to the needs of others.

Often young women ask if leadership in single life won't make it more difficult for them to be submissive to their husbands when they are married. My answer to that is simply this: if you have leadership ability you will be using it all your life. Your sensitivity to others will determine how you use it and where you use it, just as it should in single life.

Submission to one's husband is an attitude; not an act where one wears a mask and plays a part. Submission comes out of love, and love instructs us in relationships and tempers our personalities. In other words, if I am capable of responsibility before marriage, I will be capable after marriage because I am who I am. The areas in which I exert my capabilities may vary, but my abilities do not suddenly cease. The struggle in marriage is often caused by too independent a spirit, a spirit which needs to learn how to be concerned for another's well-being.

The liberated woman probably is no crusader, but she may be persistent. In the church she insists that women can do more than work in the kitchen and the nursery. She speaks quietly to a church matchmaker about her over-delight in marriages which communicate negative value to the unmarried women in the congregation. In fact, the minister has received a careful rebuke from her about 1) his jokes about spinsters and 2) his shabby handling of the text of Paul's teaching on woman being made for man.

She may take her pen in hand to protest; she may deliver speeches about the principles she believes important in women's rights, but she will not let a bitter spirit ferment within her.

As a married woman with children she is certain enough of her goals to be unmoved by the excesses of radical feminists whose definition of fulfillment automatically requires finding a job.

She may even be among the mothers who actually like having their kids around them, giving them lunch, reading them stories, talking, and knowing them as people. She enjoys being a mother and a wife. When she said "yes," she knew there would be diapers as well as roses. The crusaders didn't ask her before declaring that "all women suffer from economic exploitation, from psychological deprivation, and from exploitive sexuality." She would have cast a negative vote.

Or she may even be so liberated that she can enjoy leisure, a rare commodity in our day, and use it to good advantage. Imagine the privilege of ordering your own day and filling it with pleasures and duties you count worthwhile!

The most significant of all evidences of true liberation is the ability to love and enhance another's personhood. The angry feminist has not learned nor experienced this freedom. She does not know the awesome, expanding creativity of love. Love power is the sacred trust of those who know what it means to lose your life to find it. In a day of protesting feminists, as I observe women who seem to be really free, I see individuals who possess a peaceful spirit and find their dignity reflected in their relationship with God, not in society's trappings.

Some years ago, before the current flurry of feminists movements, Harry Reasoner did a television essay on women that was most intriguing. I remember that he admitted at the beginning that it had been written by a man, thereby avoiding controversy about the point of view represented. I do not remember all that he said, but some of the flashing vignettes on the screen stay in my mind: the wrinkled face of an old woman whose countenance shone with love; a young mother stopping on the way into a supermarket to tie a small boy's shoe, concluding the task with a kiss; the tenderness of a young woman listening to a friend. Interspersed with scenes like these was a WAC sergeant barking out commands to a platoon of women; a smartly dressed and coiffured editor of a woman's magazine giving opinions on her many telephones, her voice strident and efficient. The contrasts were interesting and intentional; it was loaded emotionally. But the loving look was a clear winner. There's a compelling strength to love.

The dispute about women in today's world will undoubtedly cause discontent in women who were neutral or perhaps not perceptive beforehand. Some will lash out in anger; others will concentrate on external means of fulfillment — and many will be open for a fresh examination of themselves. Potentially, the situation is wide open to becoming more than you now are, having more self-discipline, higher goals, a more pleasing personality, greater love, a more worthwhile life, a more directed life-style.

However, if you are a member of God's family through personal faith in Christ, God expects you to walk in the light. The Apostle John wrote in his first letter to Christians,

> God is light and in him is no darkness at all. If we say we have fellowship with him while we walk in darkness, we lie and do not live according to the truth; but if we walk in the light as he is in the light, we have fellowship with one another, and the blood of Jesus his Son cleanses us from all sin.

Light exposes, which is sometimes why we prefer to walk in darkness. It exposes darkness in us. But it also illumines what we are. We don't see shadows; we see reality.

I see who I really am as I walk in the light. I don't have to prove anything about me; I can be me. God is light; he has done the exposing and the forgiving. The roof is off between God and me. The walls are down between other people and myself. I can like myself because God loves me. I can love other people because I've accepted myself.

Loving one's self is critical to loving one's neighbor. Jesus said, "Love your neighbor as yourself." Do we not have a world full of people trying to love their neighbor while still having so much to prove about themselves?

Walking in the light means that we can forgive other people and not collect their wrongs, because we have experienced forgiveness personally. We are not easily offended because Christ reaffirms our value daily.

This is the freedom of the children of God. Down through the centuries, regardless of the political and social rights of women, the woman who has this kind of liberation was never in bondage to anyone. Real liberation means walking in the light and not being afraid.

5

Living Creatively

Two little brothers shared the same room, and every night the smallest one fell out of bed, arousing the whole household in his trauma. It happened so often that the events became breakfast-time conversation. After listening quietly for some time, the older boy finally offered his opinion, "Want to know why Timmy falls out of his bed every night? . . . He goes to sleep too close to where he gets in."

Many people have Timmy's problem. They go to sleep too close to where they got in. Dull of spirit, they feel uninteresting and act that way, too, because they went to sleep where they were, and life has grown smaller and smaller.

If I were to ask you how much wealth you had gained in the last five years, what would you say? Inner wealth, I mean. The furnishings inside that are beautiful, interesting, and enriching to others. Some people are like the two men I saw in a cartoon: one said to the other, "By the time I was smart enough to know where I was going I wasn't going any place."

Of all people in the world, the people who claim to know God best ought to be the most creative simply because they are related to the Creator. He is the innovator, the creator, the artist. Imagination finds its source in him!

Imagine being there when "the morning stars sang together" as the world was created by the word of his power. He shaped birds with their various plumage; he designed the hippopotamus and the giraffe. Light, dark, sun, moon, water, sky, clouds, earth, trees — the rose. And man in his own image.

He let Adam be a word partner with him by naming the animals. He designed the high priest's robe and the mercy seat, and equipped the artisans with his Holy Spirit. He told Solomon how to carve out the lilies at the top of the columns in the temple. This is our God.

God, the creative Redeemer — who invades our planet to deliver us from our sins and the fear of death — comes not with trumpets and royal fanfare, but as a baby. God, the adventurer.

Did you know that twenty-five percent of the Bible is poetry? In the last part of Job when God speaks he gives thirty-four verses about the crocodile and ten verses to the glory of the hippo. No wonder G. K. Chesterton wrote "God may be younger than we are!"[1]

He has never grown tired of his world. The elements are created in such a way that each sunset is an original and each snowflake is different. Every baby born is a unique person. God is forever creating and enjoying his creation. The worst thing in the world, says Clyde Kilby commenting on the creative process, is to believe that today is like yesterday.

God notices; he is observant. The Bible says he knows when a sparrow falls. Are you not of more value than they? He keeps on creating in our personal lives, too. He takes all the mistakes, all the broken places and weaves the threads of our lives into something meaningful, as we trust him.

True creativity is always linked up with God. It is part of the adventure to which God calls us. Just living in fellowship with this kind of God is the greatest of crea-

---

[1] Clyde S. Kilby — The Aesthetic Poverty of Evangelicalism.

tive adventures. As we listen and obey, the Holy Spirit infiltrates into us a likeness to Jesus Christ.

Paul Tournier says, "He calls us to an adventure of faith, difficult and exacting, but full of poetry, of new discoveries, of fresh turns and sudden surprises."

Then why are some of us so small? you ask. Our smallness comes from the desire to "play it safe." Never take any risks. Never make a new decision or trust God in a fresh commitment. We look at our own resources and say, I could never do that. Our scared littleness keeps us in a box.

Adventure or creativity — whichever word you like best — always involves risks. It involves a decision; it is purposive; it is an expression of yourself. Usually it involves others. It stretches you, so that you end up being more than you ever thought you could be. It adds the special flavor to life that makes you feel that you have a secret with God.

At this point you may be thinking of the composition of an exciting piece of music, or a new harmonic arrangement, or a painting, or a poem. And you've already said, "I can't do that." Then don't do that. Find something your own size. It may be learning how to knit; it may be flying a kite on a hillside with your son and getting the tail just the right length so that it will soar out of sight in the blue, blue of the spring sky.

Creativity is taking the stuff of life that exists and shaping it. It is to be for the moment a spark of communication between God and man, reflecting some small piece of his creative nature.

Some of my adventures do not even remotely resemble painting a picture, but they have been big experiences that demanded creativity and resources I didn't know I had. The first wilderness canoe trip into Canada was one of these. My husband and myself in one canoe; our son, Mark and Bill, one of "our boys," in another. An untried river; the equipment and the right amount of food; the skills necessary for survival. When we came to our first cataract (which looked like a giant waterfall to me), I wanted to turn around and go back. Three men let me know firmly that you don't go back on trips like this; we were committed to the river. Often when there seemed no route suitable for portage, I heard my husband say, "Pick up the end of the canoe and follow me."

The black flies ate my husband until he looked measly; the mosquitoes nourished themselves on Bill until he swelled out of shape. It rained; we fought our way through log jams, paddled for hours through marsh lowlands. But there were other days. The sun shone, and a whole beautiful world was reflected in the river. No sound, except for the song of the wind in the top of the pines, eighty to a hundred feet tall, and the dip of paddles in the stream. Birds — cedar waxwings, Canada jays, yellow warblers, redstarts. The otter; the moose; the sunset over the lake; the loon's call; the softness of decaying forest underfoot; the splendor of undisturbed wilderness. *Lord,* I thought, *you made all of this and it was here praising you long before we discovered it. Thank you for sharing it with us.*

That's one kind of adventure. I wouldn't have missed it! But I would never have gone if I hadn't taken the risk, and I might never have gone if I had known the cost in sheer endurance and misery. Think of what I might have missed!

Some people don't have children because they are too busy counting costs, evaluating the risks, and weighing the odds of failure. They will never know what they missed! No one marveling at a child conceived in love, nurtured in the mother, bearing the likeness of both parents can doubt the worth of that kind of creativity.

Excuse me for placing canoe trips and having children in the same category, but I meant to observe that some people are scared of anything that doesn't have a certain end and all the risk removed. No one can really live like that. Life itself is a risk. Yet I am surprised at the number of people who never try anything new. A new recipe. (It may not be good!) A new hairstyle. (I may not like it!) A new game. (I don't know how to play.) A new place. (I've never been there before.)

> *Come weal or come woe*
> *My status is quo.*

We seek a smooth path, without any brambles or stones in the way, a straight way without too much incline that leads us to heaven quite safely. On the other hand, God, the great Adventurer, leads us over high peaks, across rocky crags, up steep ravines, across rivers we thought we couldn't cross, and gets us to heaven all breathless, bearing the fruit of our effort and the likeness of his Son — and fit for royal fellowship.

Eric Berne, author of *Games People Play*, says, "Losers spend their lives thinking about what they're going to do. Winners, on the other hand, are not afraid to savor the present, to unpack their books and listen to the birds sing. Losers say *but* and *if only*. Winners are enlightened people who grow rich, healthy, strong, wise and brave using just three words in life: *Yes, No* and *Wow.*"

We need positive attitudes to live creatively. We cannot be encumbered by past failures. The Scripture reaffirms this by urging us to "put off" and "press on." Our sensitive egos may still smart from a risk we took that left us bruised. Bruisings of this kind come most often when the adventures have been our own selfish plans rather than true acts of creativity. But remember God is still the author of new beginnings.

I do not speak lightly of ego needs. For some people telephoning someone else is a great adventure and risk. Introducing someone can be exceedingly painful for others. These are extremes of the spectrum, but they exist. And for such the status is not so much "quo" as human safety. But we are not left to that. An infinitely creative God wants to take us out of our smallness into an adventure suitable for us. We need a positive attitude to begin. We can do it, by his grace.

I'm thinking of such an adventure in my own life. God had brought a woman into my life who was an incipient alcoholic. When life's dreariness or her personal disappointment became too much, she took to the bottle and was out of sight for days. She became a Christian and her life changed radically, and the community of those who loved her had almost forgotten, if they had even known, about her problem. Then one day a neighbor innocently said something that hit a vulnerable spot in my friend; she was angry and hurt and went home.

The neighbor tried to call, other friends tried to contact her. No answer. Her car sat in the drive, but no one could reach her. On the second day the fear grew that she may have returned to the bottle. It was decided that I was to go to her home. My assignment was a rescue adventure with God, but I was a Jonah at heart. She lived in the country and had two enormous police dogs that usually met the car. I never left my car until she called them off. Would she be there to call them off? I didn't want to go; I was scared; I didn't know what to do once I got there. My husband prayed with me and shoved me out of the house. When I arrived the dogs miraculously weren't outside; I knocked on the door; she answered and fell weeping into my arms, asking, "How do you know if God forgives you?" I was so glad I went!

I did not have a positive attitude toward any detail of the adventure, but I did have a positive attitude toward God, and that is a good place to begin. And I think the illustration points out one other helpful detail; namely, the role of encouraging friends. We can encourage others to take the risk of living creatively.

A positive attitude is inspired by a spirit of thankfulness. One of the most creative exercises a woman can do is to write a weekly theme entitled, "Why I am thankful." Thankfulness changes our negatives to positives, and transforms our liabilities to abilities. A student once wrote a thankful essay for my friend Betty Carlson. It read, "I am thankful for my glasses. It keeps the boys from fighting me and the girls from kissing me."

We need a positive attitude and a spirit of thankfulness, but we also need to uncomplicate our lives. We build stress into our own lives. I'm not suggesting that we leave the sink full of dirty dishes while we enroll in an art class, but we do need to take a careful look at our lives. The details will be different for everyone, but for most it will mean planning ahead to make our lives more orderly and disciplined. There are only twenty-four hours in any one day; make them as meaningful as possible.

We waste useful energy with self-absorption better spent on being creative.

Except for a few who are able to shut themselves off from the world, our creativity must be flexible, not selfish, and subject to interruption. Particularly is this true of women who have children at home. And if you are truly creative, you will consider even the interruptions creative.

Sometimes our creativity passes through times of darkness when some of our dross is being burned off. You may be in one of those times now as you read this. Nothing has sparkled for you for quite a while. Again, return to faith in a God who sponsors personal adventure and he will help you begin.

What might some of these adventures be? It could be as simple and big an adventure as honesty with a friend. No more role playing, but the risk, the commitment to be who you really are. Real honesty requires integrity. There is a fake kind of honesty popular today that lets people think they have the right to tell a person (with a bit of disguised anger) all the things about that individual offensive to them. It's a way of saying, "I don't like lots of things about you, so why don't you do something about it." And it's a neat cop-out for learning to love. Real honesty might well work on an offensive habit with another person out of love, but it won't make another person unduly responsible for personal hang-ups.

For instance, Sally goes to Anne and says, "I have something against you. I'm jealous of you." What does Anne do? Can she negate everything in herself that makes for the jealousy? No, but Anne can take Sally's false attempt at honesty and make it creative by helping the girl to bear her own burden before God. That's at least a creative response.

The creative risk of adventure in honesty that I first suggested is that of simply letting yourself be known in ways that are free and constructive for you and everyone else. It will undoubtedly include the interchange of letting others help bail you out of your hurts and doing the same for them. A large part of living creatively is reaching outside of your self to help someone else.

Learning to listen helps creative living. Listening may well be second only to loving as a creative act. Listening says so much to the other person about her value. (That's why listening to small children is so important.) But listening lets you hear and know the other person, and you may be surprised at the totally new ideas you encounter.

I read recently of a man who said he had never been bored with anyone. When he began to feel tired of a person, he began to ask, "What is there about the life of this person that makes them so boring?" And by the time he had finished asking questions and listening to them explain themselves he was no longer bored.

The combination of honesty and listening could be a whole new adventure in quality married life for some people. Maybe your husband has never learned how to express himself or share, and you live a lonely existence. If you claim the help of a creative God who designed people with the ability to communicate, and creatively heighten your own sensitivity to your husband, you may be in on one of the biggest adventures of your life. Certainly your prayer life will develop; you'll feel the Holy Spirit controlling your responses; and you will be surprised by more than one miracle.

Never give in to a low quality of life within the home when God, the redeemer, offers his help. One young wife telephoned to say, "Something has been happening to me. It is as if God told me that if I want things to change I am going to have to keep my mouth shut. So I've been trying, and do you know what I've discovered? When you know God you don't always have to be right!"

Another woman has grown beautiful praying for her family and creating an environment that works with her prayers. She prays, "Lord, help my husband not to be so short with Jimmy. He's so sensitive and he never gets a chance to finish what he wants to say. Help John to be more aware of this." And God does.

Making something new and creative out of family life can be a married woman's great adventure. It can also be the adventure of the single person, because the close interpersonal relationships within any living situation demand his help.

One of my great adventures as a writer has come from the families who share with me how *Honey for a Child's Heart*[2] has launched them into new adventures as families through sharing of books. Writing a book is an adventure of the riskiest sort. But after the pain and loneliness of the actual production, what joy and reward to see others learn to live creatively because I took the risk of adventure.

Setting up a reading program seems so simple an idea that one hardly thinks of it as creative. And yet books can take us on the finest kind of adventure without ever leaving the house. A good adventure takes discipline, and a well-ordered life is necessary for a reading program. Think of the potential for expanded horizons, for creative thinking, for learning something new!

I was talking about good reading to a group of mission candidates recently and one winsome young man told me later in conversation that he was a poor reader and hardly ever read a book. His story revealed unfortunate situations in first and second grade and a move to a new location in third grade where other students teased him about his inability to read. He developed a barrier against reading. He was bright and his mind retained what he heard, but he didn't like to read. It threatened his view of himself. I asked, "Have you ever asked God to help you overcome this handicap and work on it with divine help?" He thought about it for a minute, and then said, "That would be a choice kind of adventure, wouldn't it?"

Both reading and learning to read fit the category of creative living. My friend may never be a speed reader, and what he sets out to do is easier said than done. But so is painting a picture or playing a musical instrument. It will take courage and sweat and perserverance.

One of my friends declares that learning to change the way you look is a phase of creative living. She says, "God gave you your face; he didn't give you your expression.

---

[2] *Honey for a Child's Heart* (Zondervan, 1969).

Why not make it more pleasant?" For others it will be
discipline of more sleep, better and less food and a decision to stop chewing the fingernails.

Every meaningful adventure I have had has involved
doing something I believed to be the will of God. I have
been pushed out over my head in experiences so many
times that I've found myself swimming strokes I didn't
know I knew! Everything from a radio talk show to taking
a chair-lift to the top of the mountain with the intent of
skiing down! I was no pro in either event, but I did have
some exciting surprises.

I've used the word swimming metaphorically, but it
reminds me of a literal swim I once took. Geraldine had
just come to trust Christ. We were taking an Exercise and
Swim class together at the Y. Following our first day of
exercises, we jumped into the pool. She stood there for a
minute and said, "I'm scared to death to put my face in
the water, but now that I know God, I'll just say a little
prayer and float across the pool on my face." She proceeded to do just that! Leaving me, who had known God
for sometime and who always swam with my head well
above the water, standing agape. So I said a little prayer
and similarly did a prone float across the pool!

The creativity of doing what you believe to be the will
of God will more often have significant spiritual dimensions. It may be taking more time with your children,
developing a new friendship, helping someone who is
needy, or sharing your faith.

Taking seriously the fact that you have been entrusted
with the Gospel will bring you your most awesome adventures. Creatively sharing the Good News is a most
expanding experience. Every person is unique: they hurt
in different places; their capacity for intake of truth varies.
To take the great truths of God's redemption and communicate these skillfully takes creativity. We don't dump
a load of truth; we interact. We need the right words, the
illustrations that apply, the ability to listen — and God's
help. No one can ever grow dull or small or uninteresting
who grabs hold of this adventure. We have been entrusted
with the truth about God!

Living creatively is as big as creation. Don't be among those who think that all birds are sparrows and that there are two kinds of trees; one with leaves and one with needles. Living creatively means noticing, being aware and alive to the world. It involves an appreciation and drive toward excellence. It involves things, people, ideas. God is noticing all the time. Shouldn't we be just a little more awake?

6

Maturing: Growing Beautiful

Some people have trouble letting the Lord shepherd them. Being wayward and headstrong by nature, we are not always sure we need help. We have our own ideas of what looks like good pasture. And so we wander here and there.

In his *Psalm of Wandering,* Joseph Bayly captures the adventures of proud, small humanness:

> "Lord you know
> I'm such a stupid sheep.
> I worry
> about all sorts of things
> whether I'll find grazing land
> still cool water
> a fold at night
> in which I can feel safe.
> I don't.
> I only find troubles
> want
> loss.
> I turn aside from You
> to plan my rebel way.
> I go astray.
> I follow other shepherds
> even other stupid sheep.
> Then when I end up

68

> on some dark mountain
> cliffs before
> wild animals behind
> I start to bleat
> Shepherd, Shepherd
> find me save me
> or I die.
> And You do."[1]

Mercifully the Lord does intervene in our lives when we call to him and, tasting his goodness, it is surprising that we would ever stray again. Happy are those who keep their hearts fixed on the Shepherd; this is what it means to mature spiritually. The most defeating trait in our lives is our tendency to double-mindedness. We say we believe one thing, but we act on a different principle.

There can be no spiritual maturing apart from eating the food he provides for us. The Bible says that "he (God) has granted to us all things that pertain to life and godliness, through the knowledge of him who called us to his own glory and excellence" (2 Peter 1:3). God wants us to know who he is, to understand the dimensions of the salvation provided in Jesus Christ, and to be comforted by the Holy Spirit's presence in our lives. *Knowing* implies information, experience and fellowship. God has revealed himself in the written Word, the Scripture, and in the living Word, Jesus Christ. We are called to his glory and excellence. It is imperative that we *know* God.

No amount of religious exercise will substitute for spending daily time studying the Bible, and then talking with God about what we have learned. One of my friends was tucking her small son into bed one night. They had just finished praying together, and he said with sudden insight, "I get it, Mom. God talks to us through the Bible, and we talk to him when we pray. Right?" Right. Profoundly right. Imagine God's love in revealing himself, his character and his works to us in Scriptures only to find that our wayward hearts are careless in exercise of the privilege of communicating with the eternal God.

---

[1] Joseph Bayly, *Psalms of My Life* (Tyndale). Used by permission of the publisher.

An African boy, reading the Scriptures for the first time
in his own tongue, said, "This book makes holes in my
heart." God means to change the way we think and the
way we act as we respond to what we read. And this reading is no perfunctory ritual; it is interacting with God and
it makes "holes in our hearts."

A friend and I had been discussing an issue concerning
personal faith, and I read a passage from the Bible aloud
to her. She had only recently become a Christian and she
interrupted me to ask, "Does it say anywhere in the Bible
that after you have committed your life to Christ you can
understand the Bible better? Because I am comprehending
what you are reading, and I have never understood the
Bible before!" She was experiencing the Holy Spirit's
ministry in her life. Jesus has promised that the Holy
Spirit would take the truths of God and make them real
to her (John 16:13-15).

God gives us his Spirit when we trust Christ, and the
Spirit's ministry in us is to reveal truth and to enlighten
our understanding. It is characteristic of new believers to
experience the thrill of this, but it is meant to be the continuing experience of all believers. God doesn't dump
character into our hearts; he wants to make our own
muscles strong by inviting us to go on in our experience
of the knowledge of him. And he gives the Holy Spirit
to us to help us grow in ways that change our lives.
Holiness is not sentiment; it is the character of Jesus
Christ worked into ours.

Those who take their refreshment daily from the Word
of God evidence this in their lives. We don't have to an-
nounce to others whether we have spent meaningful time
with God; it is reflected in the way we think. When
some Christian pours out her heart to me and what I hear
is out of tune with the grace of God, mixed-up thinking
with bitter or anxious overtones, then I know that the
solution to her unrest will be found in an exhortation to
believe in God and return to feeding on his Word. This
remedy has proved amply true in my own experience with
God. If I don't have the right diet, my spiritual life goes
askew. My point of view turns away from God to look

at situations. Ungodly thinking is simply that — thinking without God.

God spoke through the prophet Jeremiah to warn the people of Israel about their neglect of him. His words have contemporary impact in defining our failure:

> "My people have committed two evils:
> they have forsaken me,
> the fountain of living waters,
> and hewed out cisterns for themselves,
> broken cisterns,
> that can hold no water."
>
> Jeremiah 2:13

The irony of forsaking the fountain of living water to dig a cistern of our own, only to find out it doesn't hold water. What a colossal waste of divine provision and human potential. And some people hold an empty cup up to their lips all their lives.

In Psalm 18:16 God says. "I will feed you with finest wheat, and with honey from the Rock I will satisfy you." This is God's provision for us in his person, which is revealed in his Word. He satisfies the needs of our inner beings; he guides our lives in paths of truth. He has communicated to us. The Bible is a roadmap to the King, someone once said, designed to get us to the palace instead of the garbage dump.

I cannot emphasize enough the importance of a daily time with God in the Scriptures and in prayer. The way for communication is open, a fact made possible by the death of Jesus Christ. That symbolic tearing apart of the curtain to the Holy of Holies in the temple at the time of Christ's death has given us the privilege of approaching God in Christ's name. We become like those with whom we spend time; we begin to think their thoughts after them. If you want to mature and grow beautiful on the inside, listening to God must be a daily habit.

But listening must be the "hearing of faith" that helps us put truth to work in our lives. It is not an intellectual exercise we are after, but the response that involves the whole person — the will, as well as the intellect and the emotion. We are curious beings. Some people say, "If only I could feel . . . ," and in a variety of ways they let their feelings buffet them about. The biblical pattern is always to believe $\longrightarrow$ act $\longrightarrow$ know $\longrightarrow$ feel. In other words, we act on our belief which proves itself in our experience and our feelings line up. For instance, "I don't feel I can love her but I believe I should" includes the element of feeling, of belief, of action. When these are put in the right order the statement becomes," I believe I can love her (because belief puts the resources of God at our disposal); I will act lovingly towards her; my feelings are changed as I obey God." Belief, action, feeling.

Biblical belief is not simply giving assent to a truth. The Bible says devils believe this way. Biblical belief means committing your whole weight to the truth. It means walking out on a plank, expecting it to hold — and suddenly finding it is not a plank, but the very rock on which existence rests. Commitment to truth is the essential element in belief. If I were to go to a bank and present a thousand dollar bill before the teller, I might say, "I'd like to place this in the safe-keeping of this bank," but if I were to hold on to the end of the bill she would say in return, "I will be glad to deposit it, but you must let go of the bill." It is not committed until you let go and trust the safe-keeping to the bank.

Paul wrote to Timothy with the assurance that came out of commitment,

> "I am not ashamed, for I know whom I have believed and I am convinced that he is able to guard what I have entrusted to Him until that day."
>
> 2 Timothy 1:12
> (NASV)

I am not ashamed; I have believed; I am convinced. This is the secret to the authenticity and dynamic of Paul's life.

The Christian life involves claiming what God has already given us in Christ. My grandmother used to speak of this as "claiming the promises," and that is exactly what it is. Peter writes,

> He has granted to us his precious and very great promises, that through these you may escape from the corruption

that is in the world because of passion, and become partakers of the divine nature.

2 Peter 1:4

That verse is a promise in itself. It says that we can escape the worldliness which infects us and become more like Christ by claiming the promises of God. And the Bible is alive with promises.

Corrie Ten Boom speaks of this as "writing a check on the heavenly bank." The resources we need are there for us; we need to cash in on them. She learned the validity of these resources in a Nazi concentration camp and says, "It would not be in the Bible if it were not true." Taking generously from God's provision has made Corrie Ten Boom beautiful. When you are eighty and are truly beautiful, it is not cosmetics that makes it so, but a likeness to Jesus Christ.

Maturing defined means coming to full development; maturing in experience means facing reality and learning how to handle what we see. Life is not as perfect as we would like it; our own actions have added to its imperfections. We had a plan in mind and events didn't go that way. We have two choices: to rebel against the way life is or to draw on heavenly resources, to claim some of the promises that will keep us from the "corruption of passion."

The rebels hit out against life, maneuvering on their own resources, and make their own decisions and improvements to correct the faults they find in life. Sometimes it takes on the guise of great sacrifice: the enduring, martyred woman who has given all for her family and finds not-so-subtle ways to remind them. Other times lip service is given to God, but there is little question as to who is running the show. Rebels feel trapped, make decisions based on self's needs and get themselves into trouble.

A friend was recounting her own rebellion to me. She had been chafing badly at an assignment God had given her. She knew it was his will for her, but the circumstances did not suit her. She was complaining about this in a conversation with an older friend, hoping for some sympathy. Instead, after listening to the whole tale, the friend said, "Did you know that your rebellion is as witch-craft in God's sight, and that your stubbornness is as iniquity and idolatry?" (I Samuel 15:23) That was hardly the sympathy my friend was expecting, but it was the rebuke she needed. "Suddenly," she said, "I saw God's point of view about my rebellious heart. I had been toying with rebellion, almost delighting in it. Rebellion needs to be seen for what it is!"

On the other hand, we may not want to rebel against reality, but we aren't sure exactly what promises to claim. Or we feebly claim them and make such statements as I have made, "We'll just have to trust the Lord." To which my husband remarks, "Has it come to that?" We end where we should begin!

God has already provided the resources we need; his provisions far exceed our needs. The delight of being daily in the Scriptures is that he guides us to the answers we need; he shows us the principles by which to live; he gives us the promise of his personal care.

My brother and I were talking long-distance on the phone together recently, and we were speaking of our mutual grief over our father's death and our concern for our mother. He said, "You know, I was so agitated on the inside and then God showed me something. I was reading in First Peter, *Cast all your cares on him, for he cares for you.* I noticed," he continued, "that in that second phrase *cares* is in a present tense. I don't have to go looking for God to tell him my troubles, he already knows. And he cares. He just wants me to hand them over to him because they are too heavy for me." He was encouraged and so was I. I thought of the phrase from Romans 15:4, . . . "that by steadfastness and by the encouragement of the Scripture we might have hope."

The miracle of claiming the promises of God is that they change us as well as changing our circumstances. We learn how to solve tension as the Holy Spirit works out self-control within us. Blessed are those who find out they don't always have to be right. And how pitiful are those who have no self-control, who let their emotional passions, their likes and dislikes rule their lives. They are quick to act and speak, but slow to believe that the Holy Spirit will help them in their weakness and even that he prays for them according to the will of God (Romans 8:26).

We find ourselves learning to love others we don't think we could love by simply believing and claiming that "God's love has been poured into our hearts through the Holy Spirit which has been given to us" (Romans 5:5). We aren't shut up to personal ability; his resources rescue us. If we act as we should, the feeling will follow. God's great plan is to redeem us by loving us. As his love passes through us to others the miracle of redemption happens all over again. I have known the most loveless, tense situations changed by one person who decided to love with God's kind of love.

Recently I talked with a young wife who resented her husband's involvement in his work and his often thoughtless behavior to his family. As the conversation continued it was plain to see that she shut herself away from him as punishment for his neglect. She became critical, complaining of his time away, of her children, of her home, of everything.

Because her husband was of a carefree, happy nature, this was subconsciously unpleasant to him. He did not know how to grapple directly with the tension he felt, so he avoided it. He stayed away as much as he could let his work justify. The children were trapped; they reacted by being as naughty as they could.

I made only one suggestion: that she begin scattering seeds of praise around in the lives of those she loved. I think every woman ought to keep her apron pockets full of praise and be eager to cast it abroad into fertile ground. I don't mean false flattery, but the kind of thankfulness and appreciation of another's personhood that makes others better people. It's another way to let the love of God be shed abroad in our hearts.

God always encourages us; he never discourages us. Discouragement is catching, like a dreadful plague. When the twelve spies returned to the Israelites after spying out the land of Canaan, ten of the men gave so discouraging a report, that the hearts of the people filled with fear and they lifted up their voices and cried. They utterly refused to go into the land God had promised them. Later when God gave instructions concerning the warfare necessary to possess the land, he said that the officers of the people were to ask, "What man is there that is fearful and faint-hearted? Let him go back to his house lest the heart of his fellows melt as his heart" (Deuteronomy 20:8). It takes spiritual maturity to resist the discouragement of others.

Often our discouragement is a matter of pride. We are discouraged that we are not as good as we thought we were. Either we have seen our own imperfection or it has been pointed out to us. Someone hurt our feelings, or we are lonely. We are disappointed. Arthur Glasser once pointed out to a group of missionary candidates the strategy Satan uses to discourage us. He diagrammed it as downward steps to defeat:

If you watch your own emotionally bleak periods you will find this pattern at work. Does one step need to fall into the next? Can we stop the downward pull? Yes, at any point. The remedy is the sacrifice of praise found in Hebrews 13:15, "a sacrifice of praise to God, that is, the fruit of lips that acknowledge his name."

You may not feel like praising God. That doesn't matter. Do it. Take a psalm of praise and read it until the truth leaps off the page into your heart. Take a hymnal and sing songs of praise. Is God worthy to be praised? Then praise him; the feeling will come later and his praises will pull you out of the pit.

God lets us cooperate with him in this way, exercising the muscles of our will. The Bible says, *Thou dost keep him in perfect peace, whose mind is stayed on thee, be-*

cause he trusts in thee (Isaiah 26:3). God's promise is perfect peace, but it is conditioned by our keeping our mind fixed on him. He gave us our will so that we could use it for our good and his praise.

He will not allow us to be passive in experiencing his goodness. The Bible says *let your requests be made known to God, and the peace of God, which passes all understanding will keep your hearts and your minds in Christ Jesus.* Our part: let your requests be made known. But the passage goes on: *Whatever is true, whatever is honorable, whatever is just, whatever is pure, whatever is lovely, whatever is gracious, if there is any excellence, if there is anything worthy of praise, think about these things* (Philippians 4:6-8). It's a choice we have to make. Will we be anxious and fuss? Or will we tell him our requests? Will we allow our minds to dwell on the grubby side of life, or will we furnish our minds with worthy thoughts? Maturity chooses the best in the face of stress.

But anyone who is honest and realistic knows the downward pull is strong. When life is hard it isn't easy to choose the positive, to focus our minds on God or even to think about other excellent things. We are like Peter walking on the water. We do fairly well, until we begin to look at the waves instead of Jesus. Yet we determine so much about our lives by the exercise of our wills. Elaborate all the psychological bruises that make life grim, and you are still stuck with a grim life. At some point we are left with a decision about our intentionality. What do we *intend* to do? We may sometimes have our low moments, but God will maximize our intentions.

A maturing Christian realizes that the praise-worthiness of God is the source of all joy. It is his excellence, the steadfastness of his love, the perfection of his character, his faithfulness to mankind that is the well-spring of all joy. Because of him we can know joy in an imperfect, troubled world. Our feelings of happiness which are dependent on circumstances may come and go. But joy is deep-seated; it is not dependent on circumstances. Jesus said that he wanted his joy to be in us, and that the secret of joy was to abide in him, as branches abide in the vine (John 15:1-11). Joy comes out of a relationship with God.

From the first announcement of the coming of Jesus Christ into the world, the Scriptures cry out, "Fear not" and "Be of good cheer." God is still God. He intervenes in our human affairs, and he is the source of our encouragement.

Thankfulness characterizes a maturing person. The Bible gives so many instructions about praise and thanksgiving. The New Testament is dotted with the phrase "and be thankful." In Romans 1 when men are described as choosing not to honor God as God, the description of their degeneracy adds, "neither were they thankful." When Paul instructs Christians in Thessalonica about living the Christian life he tells them to "rejoice always, pray constantly and give thanks in all circumstances; for this is the will of God in Christ Jesus for you" (1 Thessalonians 5:16-18).

Thankfulness makes people beautiful. It wouldn't hurt us to make a list of things we are thankful for and present it in our prayers before the Lord. Thankfulness lists will vary, but they may include: two bluejays on the branch outside the window, clean sheets, the yawn of a small child, fresh snow, a warm day, cold milk, a warm house, drip-dry clothes, privacy, friendships, the prayers of others. Thankfulness for small things helps us stand in awe of life.

Perhaps the hardest reality to fight through is also our greatest bondage: our need to forgive. Some people carry enormous loads of collected grievances, small hurts and large offenses. Their lives are weighted down until their vision is out of focus. Jesus died so we could lay our load at the foot of the cross. He came to make forgiveness a personal experience for everyone who would trust him. Since we have been forgiven, he asks us to forgive. No freedom exists apart from our ability to forgive others. Forgiving others is proof that we understand our own forgiveness. If God can forgive me, who am I to fail to forgive someone else?

Among the most beautiful events in human history I have witnessed have been the forgiving events that unite families and friends. Some people have never learned to say. "I'm sorry," and they are usually the ones who cannot say, "I forgive you." Those two phrases put into practice and added to "I love you" are the most freeing experiences in the world.

It takes time to mature, but some have grown old without ever making it. Those who live in this kind of relationship with God grow rich and healthy and beautiful, and those closest to them rise up and call them blessed.

7

The Joy of Being Hospitable

In today's harried world hospitality is almost a lost art. And an art it is! A beautiful, enriching art that demonstrates that giving is better than receiving. The idea is as old as the creation of mankind and comes from the heart of God. God created a hospitable world, but the disorder of selfishness increasingly makes most people feel like strangers in it. One of the saddest verses in the Bible describes the coming of Jesus Christ into the world. *He came to his own home, but his own people received him not . . .* (John 1:11). God is hospitable; he expects his children to follow his example. *As many as received him, who believed on his name, to them he gave the power to become the children of God.*

Hospitality is more than a virtuous deed to be checked off a list; it is a mind-set towards life. The word *hospitable* means receiving guests or strangers warmly and generously; being favorably receptive and open to others. It is letting people into your home and into your life, and its ministry fits our human needs.

Anyone who has experienced this kind of warm reception into a family or a home knows the refreshment it brings the spirit, especially if one is traveling, lonely or unacquainted in an area. But quite apart from being a

stranger or away from home, everyone needs to be wanted
and hospitality does that for a person. It says, "You are important to us." No one is too secure or too important not to
need these simple gestures of love. Offering hospitality
is loving your neighbor as yourself. Many people gladly
receive it, but some are reluctant to offer it to others. The
very sound of the word may produce the mental image of
work, inconvenience and stress in your mind, but if it
does you are not thinking of hospitality, you are thinking
of you.

The Jews had laws defining hospitality, "The stranger
who sojourns with you shall be to you as the native among
you, and you shall love him as yourself; for you were
strangers in the land of Egypt: I am the Lord your God"
(Leviticus 19:33, 34). Strangers sojourning with the Israelites the night of the passover in Egypt feasted with
the families, according to the rules of circumcision, and
were redeemed with Israel.

Think of the rich experience of Abraham entertaining
"angels unaware" when the Lord was on his way to destroy Sodom and Gommorah. He saw three men passing
by and ran out in oriental fashion and begged them to
stay, calling the abundant feast he prepared "a morsel of
bread," standing while they ate to show his honor. Such
hospitality still exists among nomadic peoples, and many
non-Christian cultures have elaborate rituals for the en-
tertainment of guests. In some tribal groups everything
the host possesses is given for the use of the guest, includ-
ing the honor of his wife or daughters. I question that
latter generosity! But in such cultures the woman is in
the same category as other possessions.

The availability of motels, hotels and restaurants does
not cancel out the need of hospitality as some assume.
Rather it places hospitality on a different level and makes
its practice less routine and more creative. I think of a
friend who, upon meeting a visiting professor from South
Africa, immediately arranged for him to come to dinner,
inviting others to widen his circle of friendships. After a
rented room and cafeteria food, the professor had a whole
new feel for our city and our country. What a different

kind of entertaining this is than the social obligation routine of going to dinner and then "owing" a dinner in return. The Bible talks about doing good to those who cannot return the favor.

But hospitality is like casting a pebble into a lake. The ripples go to the far shore. We were in Malaysia, attempting to visit the beautiful new air-conditioned government buildings in Kuala Lumpur. Because it was hot outside, the men in our party had neither suit coats nor ties, and both are required for entrance. As we were turning to leave, a tall turbaned Sikh approached us in the friendliest manner and asked if he could help us. He observed we were Americans and said that in his student days in America he had been so cordially received that he determined that whenever he could help an American in his country he would do it. He turned out to be a member of Parliament, and hustled about to borrow ties and suitcoats from clerks working in private rooms. They were ludicrous in fit — size 32 short on a 44 long! But nevertheless, he proceeded to give us a personal tour of the chambers of government. That remains a special memory.

I have often since thought of international students we have entertained who have gone back to similar posts of government, some of them immigration officials who may now determine policies regarding missionary visas. Hospitality is never just the meal or the bed; it is the message you give a person about his value and your own personal values in the gracious giving of what is yours.

In a rural village near our home there was an ill-kempt shoe repair shop run by a strange man whose whole demeanor betrayed the cruel circumstances of his life. He lived with his cats in the back of his shop; his fingernails and the creases in his hands and face were grimy from boot black, coal soot and no hot water; the heavy underwear at the open neck of his shirt showed the neglect of his personal hygiene. He was almost wordless, grunting out replies to his customers. Sometimes he crawled on the floor because he was not wearing the wooden legs he usually hobbled on. I was curious about him and, being new in the village, I asked old-timers about his story. No one I talked with seemed to know. He was just a peculiar man, they said.

But one of our friends, a single man who worked for my husband, moved to this village soon after and, because he possessed a quiet, hospitable spirit, he invited this man into his life. He brought him to his apartment for Thanksgiving dinner, along with a couple of friends who helped him cook his first holiday meal. They ate good food, they talked, played games and as the day wore on, our shoemaker began to relax. He could hardly comprehend a place where there was so much love, simple joy and goodness.

Eventually he told his story. He was an orphan, taken in by a farm family in Canada. He worked hard as a farm hand and more than earned his keep. One bitter cold winter day after he had done the chores, his feet wet and his body numb with cold, he returned to the house only to find the door barred. He had displeased the family and they punished him by locking him out in the cold. He pounded and pleaded to be let in from thirty below zero temperatures. His feet froze; he did not get proper care, and eventually lost his legs.

He had never known love in all his life, until our friend took him into his life and tried to tell him that God loved him — an almost meaningless concept if you had never experienced human love. A miracle took place because one single man dared to let a needy person into his life.

I mention this example because single people often feel that hospitality means having a family, a house or proper furnishings. No, it means welcoming the stranger. You can be hospitable in a dormitory room, simply by caring enough to invite someone in so that you can know her and be known by her. The generous use of your car can be creative hospitality; its facets are many.

One of the most beautiful illustrations of hospitality in the Bible is the story of the Good Samaritan. He gave himself to a wounded man who was a stranger. Unable to take him to his own home, he took him to a nearby inn and paid for his care. He was in the middle of the country when he found him, but he did what he could.

The single women I know who have the richest lives
are the ones who practice hospitality. They are sensitive
to the needs and joys of others and make room in their
lives. Given all the varieties in temperament, each woman
still has to take inventory: whom have I welcomed into
my life? For whom is my leisure time spent? Who are my
friends?

The example of hospitality that deeply touches me as
I read the Scripture is the picture of Jesus cooking breakfast for the disciples on the shore of Lake Galilee after
his resurrection. Broiled fish on a charcoal fire, and bread.
The Lord of glory cooking a meal. He cared about people's
needs. I have often thought of him as I have cooked meals
for others.

The book of *Acts* describes the fellowship of the early
church as they broke bread in their homes, partook of
food with glad and generous hearts, praising God and
having favor with all the people. Imagine what it meant
for a new convert to be invited into such a hospitable
home — the sharing, the joy, the thanksgiving to God.

The missionary outreach of the church prospered under
this kind of hospitality in the first century. In a hostile
world, travelers carrying the Good News received the care
of other believers. Paul wrote of "Gaius who is host to
me." As the church grew this may have become burdensome at times, for Peter admonishes believers to "practice
hospitality ungrudgingly to one another." Perhaps he
needed to say that because a few were doing more than
their share.

Hospitality has been part of Christian witness from the
beginning. A qualification for the office of bishop is that
he must be hospitable (1 Timothy 3:2). Widows who
qualify for special ministry in the church must have proven
their good works; they must have shown hospitality (1
Timothy 5:10). Hebrew Christians were exhorted to "not
neglect to show hospitality to strangers, for thereby some
have entertained angels unaware" (Hebrews 13:2). In
Romans 12:13 "practicing hospitality" is one of the traits
of the person who has presented his body as a living sacrifice to God. Later in Romans 16:1, Paul asks the Roman

Christians to receive Phoebe, a helpful deaconness from the church at Cenchreae who was coming to Rome. Why is hospitality so important? Because people are so important to God.

Food is an important part of hospitality, and has a way of binding people together. Seated together around the table, the barriers disappear and satisfaction radiates a warm glow. Elaborate or simple, sharing the work of your hands and what you possess refreshes others.

Preparing good tasting food is a way to show people my love, but I have learned not to make the preparation so complicated that I can't enjoy the people. I have a supply of simple, tasty recipes that are neither costly nor laborious. They give me the freedom to say, "Come home for dinner." What is pleasant to look on and good to taste does not so much require labor as developed taste buds, a creative touch — and love. One does not have to be a French chef to know that colors and texture are part of the delight of eating. And a table made pretty with a small bouquet or a candle says, "Come and be with us!"

On a gourmet cooking program on television the show's host interviewed a famous personality who commented that she thought it only worthwhile to cook well for a few choice friends because the effort was an expression of love. If she did not care about the people they went out to a restaurant. She had one thing straight. Good food says, "I care about you," but she was selfish about who she cared for. Some of the people who most need the gracious touch of carefully prepared food are the neglected, unloved ones of this world — the lonely ones who find it hard to feel at home anywhere. My heart has been warmed often by a comment or a note, sometimes received years later, that tells me this kind of hospitality is valuable. I think of one note that read, "You have taught me a lot about the love of God by serving us from your best tea cups and making the table and the food seem so inviting."

But such a ministry is not just for outsiders. Personally I feel I communicate hospitality and love to my own family by the effort of tasty food. In my book it is the inalienable right of every child to come into the house and smell fresh-baked cookies or bread or something that says, "Yum-m-m. Someone here loves me!" Husbands included, of course. Along with neighbor children, and anyone else who comes in. Homes should have a loving smell.

I am no gourmet cook, but people are welcome at our table whether they are expected or not. In hospitable homes, the joy of receiving others is catching and becomes a family project. We keep extra cans of food to be opened for unexpected callers. My husband and son both cook a specialty omelet that is hard to beat. Our bean-bacon-cheese sandwiches are winners. And homemade soup from the freezer saves the day on many an occasion. Hospitality doesn't mean *fancy*; it means *I'm glad you are here*. And anyone can help set the table or carry out the dishes!

We know what it means to travel and stay in the homes of others, so we have room "in our inn" for those who need it. I learned long ago that sheets sleep just as well unironed as ironed, and so I make having guests as easy as possible. Good pillows, enough blankets, a box of tissues, a private drinking glass and a good light to read by are items I try to provide. When the garden is in bloom I may add flowers on a bedside stand. But we've also let students sleep on the floor wall to wall, and wait in long lines for use of the bathroom. And those have been some of the merriest times.

But hospitality needs to be practiced within the family and within the home as well. It's folly to talk of receiving the stranger when little sensitivity exists within the home to the needs of family members or the apartment mate. Increasingly, families do not eat together, or if they do, their meals are hurried times where everyone is free to gulp down his food and leave the table to watch television. The larger the family, the more difficult it is to make it work, but some time should be sacred in family life when we talk together as a family and get to know what has made up the day of each member. The fellowship of food can also provide the fellowship of sharing. Jimmy does not leave the table as soon as he has finished his food because to do so would be saying that he didn't care about what happened in John's life that day. We stay together and talk. It's a habit, not a punishment.

A question was asked in a small sharing group, "What was the favorite room in your house when you were growing up, and why?" I could immediately answer, "The dinette where we ate our family meals." It was actually an old-fashioned breakfast nook — benches on the sides of the table with a stool on each end. We had to take our places in the right order and be there on time! But around that table our family members recounted their day, and sometimes my father or mother would have to grant permission to speak in turn because everyone wanted to talk at once. But we grew up knowing each other and caring.

The same principle is true for a single person living with roommates. Mealtimes can be solitary, selfish events, or they can be hospitable times of sharing of food, of getting to know each other and demonstrating concern for the other's life.

The pace of life has quickened to the point where our humanity is endangered. We are not pigs at a trough. If we have a quality life, it is because we decided to make it so. Time is not measured so much by quantity as by quality. You can pack much quality into a small amount of time if you determine to do so.

Dr. Graham Blaine, chief psychiatrist at Harvard University, complains about the use of television in our lives. He says that the most serious problem of TV is not poor programming, but that it has destroyed the average family's conversation at the evening meal. When people are anxious to see a favorite program, they hurry through the meal. He says that what happened during the day, the little things, and bigger matters are never discussed.

Hospitality begins at home.

We have alluded to a variety in temperament. There are many variables that affect people's lives: physical stamina, the number of children, ease of motherhood, nature of responsibility, or personality. Some people are gregarious and like people around; others are shy, introverted and prefer privacy. Any one of these factors can be used as an excuse to live a selfish life. Women often

paralyze themselves from creativity by comparing themselves with other people. *I can't entertain like she does so
I won't be hospitable to her.* Nonsense. We go to God to
find out what he has in mind for our style of showing
hospitality, and we do that. When we face our selfishness,
our insecurities and our hang-ups realistically we can act
as we should. Hospitality is valuable, not because of style,
but because it shows genuine love for others.

One summer we ministered in a small church in a pov-
erty-stricken area where drought ruined the only salable
crop almost annually. An older daughter and her father
invited us to their home for dinner. They didn't often
have company for dinner because the area was sparsely
populated and people saved their gas to go to the store
and to church. But these people had a warm love for
God and they wanted us to come for dinner and talk about
Jesus.

I have never felt such an overflow of joy at another's
hospitality. Bessie had taken one of her chickens — an
egg-layer, thus depleting her source of cash income — and
butchered it for our dinner. With those precious eggs she
had baked desserts on her wood stove. It was a hot day;
the house had no screens and flies swarmed on the food.
That hospitality cost Bessie and her Dad something, and
we have never felt more welcomed. Their happiness in
sharing what they had — and the Lord Jesus — will be
among our warmest memories forever.

In contrast we have been invited to homes where the
obvious effort to have us there had put the whole family
uptight. They did not so much want to share themselves
as impress us with joyless perfection. I feel that way about
fireplaces that are never used to invite someone to sit near
them. Joyless cleanliness. And the tragedy often is that
the people whose homes are most beautifully appointed
often use them the least for others. On what basis do they
justify such elaborate possessions?

I have called this chapter *The Joy of Being Hospitable.*
Is it really joy? Yes, because hospitality reflects the character of Jesus Christ. It is implicit in the outworkings of
the fruit of the Spirit in our lives — love, joy, peace,

patience, kindness, goodness, faithfulness, gentleness and self-control. (Galatians 5:22)

Welcome one another, therefore, as Christ has welcomed you, for the glory of God (Romans 15:7).

8

So You're Married

When you said "yes" to Harry, you agreed to become a homemaker. Many times since then you may have said to yourself, or proclaimed to the world, "But I didn't know it would include this!" What prompted your exclamation could be a moment of sheer bliss or a moment of discontent. You expected only bliss, maybe? Then you forgot that you were still you. You didn't know such bliss existed? Then you are unaware of God's great plan.

The commitment to be a homemaker has such enormous implications that it often takes years to realize how fascinating, how all-encompassing, how strategic your calling really is. But, you may say, I said I'd be a wife, not a homemaker. What you *really* said may include a far larger assignment than you had in mind, which is precisely why we need solid teaching about the home and the meaning of relationships.

Loving someone in marriage means more than sleeping with them. It is a total commitment of life; it is an overwhelming, lasting desire to give one's self completely to another person and to create for that person an environment in which he or she can become all that God intended him to be. It is a building relationship; both partners are happier, stronger and more fully realized than before their union.

The biblical definition of marriage found in Genesis 2:24 says that a man leaves his father and mother and cleaves to his wife, and they become one flesh. Every indication of the strong verbs *leave* and *cleave* point to the establishment of a new home, a new unit. Oneness is the goal. Creating a home is a necessity.

Both partners are committed to creating a new thing, something bigger than either of them separately. Their commitment is not just to each other; it is to the new family unit their union has created. In fact, the combined impact of the union of two people from different backgrounds, with different talents, personalities, insights, and character strengths creates something greater than either of them can know at the time. One flesh becomes more rather than less; its sum total is greater than its parts.

Creating the environment, the climate, the quality relationships in which this new union will flourish is the calling of a homemaker. It is not the wife's job alone, but by the nature of her gifts, which include child-bearing and motherhood, she cannot avoid her larger responsibility in this task.

What comes to your mind when you think of the word *home?* If your response is a feeling of safety, of belonging, of love, of acceptance — then you have experienced home, and you have the necessary framework for being a homemaker. If your reaction to home is one of unhappy memories, quarrels, rejection, and attacks on your personhood, then you will appreciate new dimensions of the importance of home, but you may have to make an even greater commitment to create this positive kind of home because you have not had a model. I have observed often that those who complain most bitterly about their home background do not make the commitment and effort to change the pattern when they set up their own homes.

Home and family are under attack in today's world. Magazine articles and panel discussions debate the relevance of the institution in a technological society. Are there not other meaningful ways for people to live to-

gether? Why should mothers have to be stuck at home
with their children? Don't children thrive as well in day-
care centers? And what about communal living? The past
failure of families to live in the healthy, godly relationships
spawn such questioning. Lost people are looking for answers that will help them avoid the commitment they
have never experienced and are afraid to face.

Home and family are the basic building blocks in society,
and are God's idea. I am increasingly convinced that we
ignore their importance to our peril. If people will not
commit themselves in the most important relationships in
life, is any other commitment valid? The influence of the
home outstrips any other in the world. That it should so
often be negative in our day says nothing about the vitality
of the institution, but a great deal about us.

The home is the most convincing evidence in the world
of the reality of the Gospel. Here we can see people living in relationship to each other in a way that enhances
their personhood, loving each other, solving conflicts,
serving one another and obeying God. But this kind of
home doesn't develop by accident or with our left-over
efforts; it takes genuine commitment.

Recently I was invited to speak to a *Family Living*
class at a large university. I went with some trepidation
because I knew neither the professor nor the subject matter already covered. I found the usual cross-section of people characteristic of a university: men, women, the carefully unkempt, the anti-establishment costume-wearers, the
neatly dressed and well-combed, the open-faced, the reluctant, the friendly and the sullen. A classroom full of
individuals, a motley crew indeed. Why were they enrolled in *Family Living?* Some evidenced studied disin-
terest as I began; one had his head down on his books
feigning sleep. After some introductory remarks I began to
discuss a definition of home. I said, "A home is a safe
place. It is a fortress where its members are free from
attack. Though each is different, the personhood of each
is affirmed. . . ."

I finished the first sentence, and suddenly everyone was
at attention, looking at me. *A home is a safe place.* Soft,

hungry, wistful looks in those eyes that turned toward me. Something emotional was happening in that classroom, and observing it, I felt a sword of compassion stab my heart. Every single person in that room wanted a safe place! It was written on their faces.

Later I led a discussion on my presentation and I heard remarks like: *I've been looking for a safe place all my life. . . . What makes a home safe? How do you begin?*

It begins with a commitment to build something bigger than yourself — that meets more needs than those of your own small fitfulness. It will take the very best any woman has to offer. It cannot be her casual interest; it must be her major concern. It will drive her to a life with God that is deep and rich and will mean the unconscious expansion of her puny soul. Being a homemaker is the great adventure God entrusted to a married woman, and her influence spreads beyond her imagination.

We live in a merchandising climate today; if a thing doesn't bring in money, its worth is doubtful. Housewives or homemakers, as I prefer to call them, are not paid for their work in dollars, and money is the mark of value in our society. Strong pressure from a variety of quarters makes a young mother doubt whether it really is making good use of her education to stay at home tending a two-year-old and a new baby. "I have a master's degree that is just going to waste." If our idea of education is so utilitarian, I doubt if we have any appreciation of its value. Since when is education only designed to bring in money? I thought it was to provide some inner wealth in terms of *being.*

I stand up in this age of uncertain values and proclaim a homemaker's right *not* to have to work outside the home. She can moonlight[1] if she wants to, but her real job is at home. Being a homemaker is no small task, and the woman who believes that she can carry on two equal careers at once is only fooling herself. A career is one thing; moonlighting is another. I do some moonlighting

---

[1] Moonlighting — the extra work or interest taken up in extra time after one's real job is finished.

myself upon occasion, but I am convinced that it is only worth the stress on family life if the whole family profits by it, rather than just the wife herself. And that calls for a tight, wise value judgment that should be reviewed often.

Obviously, some women have to work because the support of their families depends on them. How happily most of these would give up dual responsibility if they could! And others work to help put children through college and for a variety of worthwhile reasons. Working is not the issue; our motivation and sense of purpose is.

It's almost become a new gospel: if you want to be fulfilled and have your dreams realized, get outside employment. And with women over a third of the nation's labor force, the working wife is a fact of life. Yes, women have the right to work, but they also have the right not to work. Another question needs to be raised. Are rights the issue?

I regard the profession of a homemaker too highly not to sound a warning lest a great calling go unappreciated — a calling which profoundly affects our society.

I know all about the mothers who are frustrated career women — who have to live vicariously through their children. I know about the club women, the over-volunteered who neglect hearth and home seeking fulfillment apart from a job. There are many ways to be self-centered. You can prove almost anything from a survey if you word the questions right, and if you ask the right people. Only recently I read a survey that claimed that the role of wife and mother meant sacrificing self-esteem, a deficiency which showed up in middle age, while the career woman had a growing sense of self-worth. Married career women viewed themselves as better mothers and more attractive to men than non-working wives, which proves exactly nothing. It might just be that working women are more aggressive in justifying their actions by "viewing themselves" as superior. The process is called rationalization.

Terrible examples come out of real life to support the to-work-or-not-to-work debate. Doing some moonlighting may help a woman keep her point of view. Let her do that if it seems right. But choosing up sides and voting doesn't give us the answer. We need God's perspective on a larger commitment and His personal direction for our lives. He judges our motives, and it is here that we stand and fall. If our goal is simply the luxury of two incomes, wanting to feel important (instead of *being* important to a few) or having to prove our worth — then God has some more basic, eternally satisfying ways to meet those needs.

Our problem is not so much lost identity, as the propagandist would have us think, but of lost goals. And the lost goals are evidenced in divorce rates, in delinquent, confused children and in our shallow, meaningless lives. We need to conduct our lives on the basis of reality, not on the data found in magazine articles or surveys.

The first duty of wife/homemaker is to know her husband. Every marriage is a unique combination of two personalities. We might need to add *of two people who are sinners* because sometimes the blinding glare of love leads us to believe that *eros* has transported us beyond our faults. Given all the differences that exist between two people, that oneness of purpose and action can occur in a marriage is proof of the grace of God. But it is so often the little foxes that spoil the vines: *he doesn't hang up his clothes; he leaves the washcloth in the sink; he doesn't wipe his feet.* O for the wisdom to know the difference between what is important and what is trivia. Every woman needs to learn how to distill the sweetness from the mixture of every day's experiences. Otherwise her attention to detail can become so perverted that she may consider her husband the enemy of her household — which scarcely qualifies as making a home for someone. Some women are more in love with neatness than with their husbands.

Knowing a person is the adventure of marriage. Partners rarely come together with highly developed skills in self-disclosure. Knowing your husband means observing his habits, his likes and dislikes — but it goes beyond that. What makes him uptight and what comforts him? How does he think and what does he feel? Notice that the list moves from the less complicated to the greater understanding. If we fail in comprehending and ministering in the area of the simple, what are our chances for success in the complex? For instance, granted that a man can learn how to hang up his pajamas, a wife can make such a big deal out of this that she closes him off from any deeper level of communication.

Individuals are programmed differently. I'm a turnip in the morning. I roll up into a ball and want to stay underground for a while. In contrast my husband wakes with a song. Every day is beautiful for him and he moves with vigor into it. If he takes more than eight deep breaths at night before falling asleep, he thinks he has insomnia. More often than not, I lie and re-do my day before falling asleep. When I was a new bride (he has managed to make me feel like a bride for years) I sometimes woke him up because I felt he had deserted me and I was lonely. We laugh about that now because it resembles a television commercial.

But his habits have been good for me. I've come to love his cheery whistle coming from the bathroom while I shake myself out of my drowsiness. And he has long since given up the idea that I will bound out of bed first, if indeed he ever expected it. I know he likes a big breakfast, and he wants to begin the day with everyone around the table. And so this is what we do at our house, and as I listen to him read the Scripture and pray for the details of the day each one faces, I'm grateful he had the warm good sense to insist on living this way.

But another husband may be the opposite. He may not want to speak until twenty minutes after his first cup of coffee. You may want to discuss all the things you forgot the night before over breakfast. Adjustment is necessary for both people in a marriage, and it comes with knowing each other, talking about living together and a decision not to bump into a person where they already hurt. And hurts do heal and living patterns do change. That's what growth is all about.

I remember hearing a story of a man, speaking to his wife on his deathbed. He said, "Honey, just before I go I want to tell you one thing. I really haven't minded eating all those chicken livers you gave me ever since we were married, even though I hate chicken livers."

"O dear," she said, "and all these years I have watched you eating them and wished I could have them!"

That's a classic illustration of poor communication. God gave us speech so we could talk, and most marriages need help on the level of better communication. Never be content with low quality in this area. A creative God wants to draw us out of our aloneness into the joy of fellowship. But some women are guilty of over-kill with their verbal skills. It's called nagging. And it does kill husbands; it kills their desire to communicate.

"A little more carrot and a little less stick" is an old proverb for getting along with donkeys. And while not wanting to put husbands and donkeys in the same league, it is a principle of life for homemakers. Husbands thrive on love; so do children. The creative homemaker finds many ways to scatter love around in her life, and finds its rich dividends returning to her.

The Bible uses the marriage relationship to illustrate the relationship God has with his people. Israel is called the wife of God in the Old Testament; in the New Testament the Church is called the bride of Christ. These analogies profoundly instruct us in our Christian life and in our married life. For instance, imagine Christ abusing the Church or being unfaithful to her. Or the Church refusing or accusing Christ. The quality of earthly relationship is elevated by the mystery of our quality relationship with the living God.

But perhaps the most familiar biblical passage about marriage is also the least understood. Paul gives instructions about relationships in his letter to the Ephesian church. His theme is the unity found in Christ. He instructs Christians in practical relationships between husbands, wives, children, parents, employees and employers. He begins by teaching that all Christians should be submissive to one another (Ephesians 5:21); that is, they should receive encouragement, exhortation, rebuke, instruction from one another because this kind of humility marks those who belong to the Christian family.

Then he goes on to give the instructions read at almost every church wedding ceremony: *Wives, be subject to your husbands, as to the Lord. For the husband is the head of the wife as Christ is the head of the church, his body, and is himself its Savior. As the church is subject to Christ, so let wives also be subject in everything to their husbands* (Ephesians 5:22-24). With an angry glint in the eye, many contemporary women accuse Paul of perpetrating his prejudices to their advantage. I object to their accusation because their presupposition about marriage is based on togetherness, not oneness, and there is virtually no comprehension of the context of the instruction nor the ideal behind it.

Someone has to be the leader. God gave that role to the husband. It does not necessarily mean that he has superior intelligence, wisdom or ability; it simply means he is responsible to God for the family. This being so, God's instructions (and I believe they are God's instructions given through Paul) are that wives should be submissive to their husbands, as to the Lord. In other words, don't compete for headship. Make it easy for your husband to become what God wants him to be. Just because he is a man doesn't mean he is naturally buoyant with self-confidence. Don't destroy his leadership. Hold him to his highest. Your submission says nothing about inferiority or superiority, just as his headship is no comment on his. It is simply fulfilling responsibility.

Notice, too, that the instructions do not say "be submissive *if* he loves you as Christ loves the church." It says be submissive in everything as to the Lord. That does *not* mean that you never have an opinion, a complaint or an original idea. Some men have used this instruction as a put-down for their wives, keeping them uninformed about important family affairs and acting as if their wives were mentally incompetent. That is not even implied in this passage because of its emphasis on oneness. God holds such men responsible for egotistic, domineering leadership which does not reflect his own character. The instruction for the husband to love his wife as Christ loved the church — sacrificially (He died for her), purposefully (He has a high goal in mind for her), and willfully (His love knows no whims) — precludes this kind of behavior.

But that is the husband's problem, not the wife's. The wife's problem is that she is often willful and competitive, so aggressive and verbal that the husband abdicates his leadership, believing the wife can run the home and family better anyway. And no wife is *really* happy with that ·arrangement. A happy marriage experiences a mutuality, an enhancing, a oneness that reflects the character of God.

The verbal skills of some women intimidate some men and cause them to clam up. That becomes both the man and the woman's problem to solve together. He needs to be less threatened and carry on with leadership under God. She needs to be more cautious in her speech. But articulation does not equal leadership, as some assume. Character strength and personal integrity are the real tests of leadership.

The home must have order; there must be a leader. But a good leader is not a dictator, and a man's wife is his best consultant. In that sense they make decisions together. We are simply foolish if we do not admit to a hierarchy of leadership or order in the universe itself. It exists within the Godhead. Jesus said he always did the will of his Father in heaven, and was subject to him. Did this diminish Christ in any way? I think not.

The whole discussion of relationships in Ephesians 5 and 6 is vitally important because high goals undergird all the instructions. They are not meaningless, rigid laws designed to make our life hard. God has a high goal in mind for wives, for husbands, and for children. Could the lack in male leadership in the world somehow reflect on what some women have done to their husbands and sons? A good teacher gives instructions in the areas where it is most needed! And God is a good teacher.

Too few married people sit down and establish adequate goals for their marriage. The home becomes a battleground where each grabs to fill personal needs, abusing the other. No woman who is consumed with filling her own emptiness and inner need can make a home for anyone else.

She's too immature. Her myopia keeps her from seeing beyond her own needs.

Often in the battles of such a home one person is exploited by the other and becomes a shell instead of a person. Sometimes a husband rules the roost with cocksure opinions, relegating his wife to the servitude of providing for his needs, negating her person. Even more frequently the wife becomes the domineering, possessive one, relegating her husband (and her children) to a spineless existence. Whatever the case, such marriages reduce the strength of both persons below their separate strengths.

Another kind of marriage may equal the separate strength of both the man and the woman. Each pursues a separate goal, going his individual way. Two people live together in the same house, but are not involved in each other's life in any way which changes the individual's potential. The contemporary Women's Lib movement fosters this as ideal, as true liberation. The partners remain free agents, each pursuing his own course. I believe this falls short of the biblical ideal, and confines each person to the prison of self.

The *one flesh* concept soars off to greater heights than this. Both husband and wife work toward goals they set for themselves as a unit. Each is more fully realized as they operate as an entity. They are building something bigger than themselves, involving the will of God for their life together. Both husband and wife are liberated in this kind of marriage.

Children who are born into this kind of home are already enrolled in a head-start program. They are less likely to become pawns in the play-off between husband and wife, because everyone is playing on the same team. And there is a game plan. The family has already decided what is valuable, what is worthwhile, and which road to take.

Being a homemaker for children is the second delight of a woman. Their whole view of life will be conditioned by your creativity in this role. Their view of God, of safety, of forgiveness, of love, of loyalty — and thousands of other attitudes will come from you and your husband.

By sheer virtue of the close relationship necessitated by care, you will influence them most. You will furnish their spirits with the concepts out of which they will build their lives.

After cleaning up a mess for the fifth time in one day, it is a rare young mother responsible for a couple of pre-schoolers who does not feel like abandoning everyone and going off on a Caribbean cruise. And she doesn't have to pretend she doesn't feel that way. Her husband, in the pressure-cooker of his job, may wish he could escape having to earn a living and run away to climb the Alps, too. That's the stuff life is made of, and our commitment to a quality life provides the ballast to keep the ship on course.

To bear and rear children is to take on both joy and sorrow, but this is the heart of living. It is folly to compare its satisfactions with a career simply because the two do not bear comparison. To present to the world and to the church a covey of people who know how to live and who are not threatened by the world is a gift to humanity beyond comparison.

But the danger for the homemaker is that she will lose her sense of humor and begin to take on super-mother qualities in her zeal to do a good job. Self-consciousness can make us try too hard and we can mutilate both our marriage and our children. Probably the biggest boon to raising children is our own mental and spiritual health. We need to learn that fussing doesn't do as much as praying, that consistency is a gem of rare beauty, that discipline and allowing appropriate independence are part of growing up. Loving will mean standing with one foot in the child's life and one foot in the realities of a hard world, for the person who loses the child inside her is in no shape to teach anyone about the world.

A homemaker realizes that she is making the home for people, not for pages in a magazine. The compulsive housekeeper has to remember that perfection is not the goal; wholeness and a comfortable sense of well-being come first. Nothing can kill her joy more quickly than jealousy over what someone else has. *How can they afford that?* has spoiled the splendor of many obvious personal blessings.

But, having said that, a child deserves to grow up in an atmosphere of beauty. And he needs to learn that everything in life is not for his use. Be such an atmosphere ever so simple and inexpensive, the homemaker has the freedom to create this kind of environment. A vase of forsythia being forced to bloom in early March, a candle on a low table, flowers on a sick tray, pictures rightly arranged, a place for things that seems just right. Things to admire, things not to touch, things that make the room seem cozy and warm. In my mind, being a homemaker can be the most creative job in the world, and I have great admiration for young mothers I know who surround those they love with a charm that was first born in the heart of Eve.

Phillips Brooks said, "Duty makes us do things well, but love makes us do them beautifully."

A woman can grow beautiful and strong being a homemaker. Potentially the position can bring out the best in her because it will tax and test all her resources. But it can also provide the opportunity for her to grow small and petty. It's like any other job in that respect. A woman can regard her children as possessions and harry them to distraction with her demand for perfection or performance that matches the neighbor's children. Her obsession with her house can make her a complaining nuisance. Her jealousy of her husband and her unwise intervention can create a continual feud. She may be so involved with the children that she neglects her husband completely. She can grow unaware of the trials and temptations of his life, and fail to hold him to the commitment of their common goals.

If she compares herself with others, she is bound to suffer defeat. She has to like herself and believe in her natural abilities to do the job. She may not be clever in one area, but she can excel in another. Elsewhere in the world, people take differences in natural ability for granted. Somehow within the home, the woman often believes she has to be a super-person. Personalities differ, so does natural wisdom. The size of the family alone makes demands on a woman, and some women find motherhood easier than others. Success comes in different shaped packages to those who accept themselves and are wise enough to hang on to the resources of God.

Part of the stress on a homemaker's life derives from her constantly changing role. First she is a bride, learning the basics of relating to her husband; then she is the mother of small children who need much attention; in the next phase she finds herself involved in lessons, in baking cookies for a school party, in transportation; then suddenly she doesn't feel as needed as she once did and she struggles over her children's independence. She may even make the mistake of believing she is no longer needed, and become too busy to observe and listen, losing communication with her children at a crucial point in life. Time goes on through a series of phases, and suddenly the nest is empty and she is back to the days of being a bride. Happy is the woman who has managed to stay a bride, a lover, through the years. And happy, too, is the woman who has managed to maintain her own sense of personhood during all the years when she gave herself so generously to others. She will know the gracious way to use the leisure now given her.

Seeing the stress and the changes in homemaking, some opt for an easier course, trying to beat off the hazards. But hazards are numerous on other roads too, and the joys are fewer.

I came across a prayer that seems appropriate for homemakers.

> *Lord, Teach us to be twice as tough*
> *and twice as tender as only*
> *the truly tough can be tender.*

9

A Worm in the Apple

Life for the single woman has never looked better. Professionally she can enter almost any field her abilities and inner drives might inspire. The career girl is definitely a positive concept in today's world. She often owns her own car, has her own apartment, and has the freedom to order her life without having to take others into account. An aura, a mystique hovers over the career woman.

But that's only half the story. The single woman must still battle the instinct of her heart and body, the injustice of discrimination and, in today's world, a feminist raid on her value system. If she is restless, there is irony in her discontent. Clearly there aren't enough men to go around: 109 women to every 100 men. And some of the women who have the men seem strangely unhappy with the idea of belonging to them. They complain of having lost their identity, while it may seem to the unmarried women that society is structured to give identity only to the married. There's a worm in the apple no matter where you bite!

"Little girls want to be princesses, but little boys don't want to be princes," writes Sydney Harris, "and from those two different starting points come all the confusions, contradictions and cross-purposes of courtship and marriage." And we might add — non-marriage.

Many single women have to wrestle repeatedly with the longing to be married. Loneliness is very real. It is hardly an issue one settles once for all. A woman generally has a stronger sense of personal bond than a man, and linking her life up with the right man makes sense to a woman. Observing this, some have categorized women as dependent, which is not necessarily so. Dependency has different connotations than the innate desire to be part of someone else. A desire to give herself is part of a woman's genetic make-up.

Handling this inner longing presents a problem to the single woman. She may often feel frustrated and even angry at God for her spinsterhood. She may feel deprived of sex and motherhood. She may not be sufficiently career-oriented to find natural satisfaction in other roles. She resents a society where males have the privilege of initiative, and females must wait to be asked. But she has to feign contentment. If she allows her disappointment at being unmarried to show, she is the brunt of jokes and ridicule from others. Others sympathize if she sorrows over a lost love, but if no dashing cavalier, whether bold, fat or handsome, has ever appeared on the scene she must carry on as if she didn't care. In fact, society asks her to be super-human about her disappointment.

Fortunately, the road has turned so that open, honest admissions are easier and the world offers a variety of opportunities and personal fulfillments. The single woman looks around and cannot help seeing a disproportionate number of restless, frustrated married women. If she is wise, she probably will question what *does* make a woman happy anyway. It is true that we tend to be dreamers, however. We often envy the privileges of others and are sure we would never have their difficulties. The single woman who wants to marry is not comforted by the failures of others. We take only positive examples when we make our comparisons and complaints. That's human optimism, and it's a good thing. Offering consolation to a single woman by suggesting that at least she's avoiding the unhappiness of *some* marriages may only show you don't understand her predicament.

Somewhere along the line women ought to catch on that marriage does not automatically equal happiness. But it may still seem like a pleasant out from a world where personal female value is computed by the relationship a woman has to a man. Woman's role has been wreathed in myth. In some ways it is true she is a prisoner of male imagination and male interpretation of theology. Failure for a woman in some circles is not to be chosen by a man. And when women are discriminated against in job opportunities and in paychecks, it is no wonder they have negative feelings about their womanhood.

Men don't spend much time worrying about being men. (My favorite man says that perhaps if they spent more time doing so they'd make it easier for women!) Men categorize women and decide what they can do and what they can't do. They often echo the arrogance of Henry Higgins, "Why can't a woman be more like a man?" Despite freedom hardly known elsewhere in the world, it's not too surprising that all the introspection and discussion about womanhood has caused the female members of the human race more anxiety, depression, and even more suicides than ten years ago.

We have to stop letting society — and the news media's interpretation of male thinking — tell us who we are. Our self-view is critical. The only relationship that defines our worth is the one we have with God. Every woman should have the chance to be her unique self without the trappings and trimmings of psychological hang-ups or society's pressures. She not only has the right to be an individual; she has the obligation to be one. She cannot make any useful contribution to life unless she does. After all, the purpose of life is to live it eagerly and without fear. The single girl may long to be able to sign her name "Mrs. Ted Jones," while the married woman fusses about having no identity other than "Ted's wife" or "Sara's mother." Both positions are ridiculous. It reminds me of a song, *you only want it 'cause you haven't got it.*

When the Bible refers to women it usually speaks about married women. This is the norm for women in any society. But can you take phrases which refer to married women and paste them on unmarried women? For instance, in Genesis when God speaks to Eve about her future, he says, "Your desire shall be to your husband and he shall rule over you." What does this say to the unmarried woman? In Ephesians 5:22 and First Corinthians 11:3, wives are to be submissive to their husbands and under their headship. While a general principle of the headship or leadership of man exists throughout Scripture there seems little basis for saying that all women must be submissive to all men. Rather both men and women are urged to be submissive one to another (Ephesians 5:21) thus displaying the Christian graces of humility and love, and reflecting their common submission to Jesus Christ.

I think it is safe to say that women *want* leadership from men, and part of their rebellion comes at the failure of men to act responsibly. Many a dominant, nagging wife is secretly crying out for the man to do what he ought to do. But leadership is different than lording it over the woman. Paul says that the whole plan is God's idea and male and female share dependent relationships (1 Corinthians 11:11, 12). This needs to be said because some gifted single women get hung-up on playing a role instead of being a person.

Women are exploited emotionally about physical beauty. Badgered by Madison Avenue's manipulation of a natural desire to be attractive, women go through painful anxieties over their appearance. I admire the present youth culture for their insistence that if beauty is only skin deep, why not insist that ugliness is only skin deep, too. The young tend increasingly to look beyond appearances to find the person underneath. But let's face it. Another part of the world still turns its head only for beauty and responds to the tug of physical attraction.

And that's not all bad. Every woman ought to look as good as she can. Sloppiness is no virtue; neither is a head of hair that needs a good styling job. Perfume smells better than body odor. Too many rolls of fat are neither healthy nor pretty; and a scrubbed-looking face is pleasanter than an overly-painted one. Looking our best makes us stand taller and gives us more confidence. Our mistake comes when we derive our value from our physical appearance. If we believe that an unattractive nose makes an unattractive person we've lost the battle at the first pass. Don't be found hating thick ankles more than an ugly soul!

More important than beauty is the reputation of your person. What words do people use to describe you? What words would you like them to use? The discrepancy in your answers may indicate what your priorities should be.

All women are potentially selfish simply because they are human. The hazards for single women to become rigid and self-centered are greater. The married woman will have her selfishness contested by both her husband and her children. If she doesn't outgrow it, she leaves a scar on more than one life. The disaster for the single person comes when she retreats from inter-personal relationships and increasingly grows inflexible, opinionated, set in her ways and miserably self-centered.

Some women are neurotic; they may need to change either their job or their outside interests. Others have sharp, shrill voices; they need to relax inside and learn how to laugh and play. Some women come into any friend's life like a two-ton Mack truck; they need to examine what dominance-need makes them act this way. Some women have trouble loving, and need to learn the freedom love brings.

But many women grow older and single with quiet good humor and rich lives. They spread love and light and joy around because they have a large supply of it inside. They enter the lives of others with an easy grace. They are interesting, loving human beings who aren't obsessed with their singleness. Men like them; so do women. Usually they have a high calling and are doing what they enjoy.

These women have not let marriage define life for them. They are confident of their personal worth and live with a wholesome awareness and aliveness to the world that belies the stereotyped image of the spinster. No one pities them because their life is wide and full and rich.

In fact, the kind of single women I am thinking about

could rightly be called sensuous. *Sensuous* is a word that
needs to be rescued from purely sexual connotations. To
be sensuous means to be present in every moment of life
— feeling life, enjoying it, learning, exploring, appreciating
the world God made and the people in it. It is simply
to be alive in one's senses.

Many of these women have given themselves to large
purposes in life. They may feel called by God not to
marry to fulfill the task, to use the gift, to finish the job.
In short, they are caught up in an adventure larger than
their own life, and in the end this is what makes life
significant and fulfilling for anyone.

In particular, women have done an incredible job in the
mission of the church with an enthusiasm and a dedication
that puts men to shame. Women counselors, teachers, doctors, nurses, translation specialists, writers — the list of
noble achievements is known only to God. The important
factor for us to observe is that these women have linked
their life up with God and the ultimate meaning of the
universe. Anyone who looks at such a woman and be-
moans, "What a pity she didn't marry!" has a small view
of what living is all about. From my point of view, I'd
rather ask a question about the judgment of the men who
passed up these noble women to choose an often shallow,
self-centered woman instead. But I am content to let God
be the Sovereign who calls such women into adventure
with himself.

It is true to say that the single woman has a difficult
task. She must adjust to hope. She must be prepared for
marriage if it comes and for singleness if it remains. Some
women decide that they do not want to marry and settle
into a single life. They do not live with either the joy or
sorrow of expectancy. Others take matters into their own
hands and maneuver for marriage, sometimes with a
panic that lacks the dignity of personhood. Whichever
the case, women can cut themselves off from the surprises
of God. The "resigned" woman, whether married or single, lacks the vibrancy that expectation brings. And if a
woman knows a creative God she may be in for all sorts
of surprises.

Why do you want to marry? is an important question. Marrying for the wrong reasons has brought all the miseries the single girl can't avoid noticing. Grabbing at marriage to fill inner emptiness soon reveals that marriage is a false god. Marriage does not change one's essential character or nature. Nor is it a happiness button. A second question, Are you becoming the person the kind of man you want would marry? We keep wanting to conjugate the verbs *to find, to want, to do,* forgetting that the most important verb is *to be.* What you are becoming is vitally important.

Reasons for marriage usually fall in the category labeled *human* or *emotional* or *physical.* Safety, protection, companionship, provision, sex, status — the list could go on. But the list is only valid for a Christian when the larger spiritual factor is taken into consideration: Is this marriage the will of God? And the will of God lines up with the principles of marriage found in the Scripture.

Which brings us to the point of the goodness of God. God's will is never second best; his will is always first best! To define for God the only way you can be happy is to say you don't really believe in either his goodness or his love. And when life isn't going according to our dreams, it's easy to ask, "How can a good God do this?" The Bible assures us that He calls each of us by name; all the "walls" of our lives are clearly known to him. The first step to real life is always hooked up to our relationship with God. If we do not believe we are loved by him we can go on an endless search for love. It is not idle, easy talk to say that our most profound contentment is found in Christ.

If she fails to believe in the goodness and love of God, strange things can happen to a woman. She grows brittle inside. Blaming external circumstance for lack of fulfillment or frustration, she uses the cutting edge of sarcasm to make her way through life. Or she becomes uptight, a kind of pseudo-woman, domineering and brusque. Harboring resentments, making mountains out of mole hills, she throws her failures on someone else. She begins to live against the world. It's the dread disease of dissatisfied womanhood.

Every woman has to work through her own set of barriers. She cannot do this as long as she refuses to face reality. A woman's challenge is to make a success either of one's celibacy or one's marriage. Both require effort, commitment and development of inner resources. If a woman spends her time dreaming only of what could be or living in an unreal existence, she ceases to live in the *now*. And no one is attracted to an empty shell. You don't start living when a man comes into your life; you have to live *now*. You have to be someone worth knowing whether married or single, if life is to be rich.

But what about sex? you ask. Every magazine you pick up features either articles or advertisements of books or products elaborating the importance of the sexual experience. Never has history known such diligent struggle over the orgasm. It's like a strange cult. Everything you've ever wanted to know or experience studied in a laboratory. Sex becomes the *summum bonum* of life. And I've heard women say, "It would be terrible to die never having known a man sexually." And some have sold their souls for a cheap experience. The woman's right to an orgasm has become a tenet of militant feminism.

We do have a sex drive. Admit it. You can talk to God about it, since he gave it to you. Sexual desire is real. But no one has died yet from perpetual virginity, and sublimation does not scar the psyche. Sex is not a basic human need; love is.

Mental and physical health demand that we act wholesomely on this point and refuse to buy the world's point of view. This may mean that upon awaking we refuse to lie in bed thinking sleepy, erotic thoughts. We learn how to discipline our thought life and we plan a program of physical exercise to work off some steam, just as men do who make a commitment to chastity.

Because of propaganda that over-estimates the worth of the sexual experience as a thing in itself, some women have fallen into the trap of masturbation. Affluence provides privacy, and for those looking for a phony thrill, the magazines even offer manipulators for sale. The woman who thus involves herself in self-love digs a pit for herself that only has a miry bottom. Increasingly normal relationships lose their value and a sickness of self-absorption destroys one's self-respect. It's the devil's lie because it says that God is cheating you from what you need; you have to supply your own needs. Playing dumb is no feminine virtue; neither is playing with yourself or exploiting some other female in the game called lesbianism. Beware of propaganda that suggests worship at the wrong shrine. The wise woman looks beyond momentary satisfaction to ask "What will I be like at 65?"

Never be content with trivia. You can squeeze your heart dry over nothing. The attitude of faith is the only truly human one because it gets us beyond ourselves and focuses our attention on the purpose in the universe. We can be conscious of doubts, but we need to be more conscious of God. We need to get our approval, our sense of being loved and worthwhile from him, not from the response of those around us.

A pessimistic spirit plagues some women, and it makes them afraid to live or try anything new. I've tried skiing and as soon as I think I'm going to fall, I fall. It's like the verse in Proverbs 22:13 where the sluggard says, "There is a lion outside! I shall be slain in the streets!" Stay inside. Wait, don't live.

In the final analysis, whether a woman is married or single, she has two choices: either to live her life reluctantly or with conviction. If she lives it with conviction she will find an outlet in life, a way to use her energy, her love, her gifts, her mind — her totality — in a way that will bring deep fulfillment. A single woman who thinks marriage is the only worthwhile adventure is going to have a shriveled life. She needs to like what she is doing now. And with all the choices in the world and given a creative God, it isn't likely that a person cannot find a niche in life that already has her name on it. It may be a growing niche, but she won't find it if she lives like a butterfly, flitting from place to place, unwilling to commit herself to the discipline of self-discovery.

For some this will be working in partnership or assisting a worthy man, making a contribution to his work, enjoying his friendship and the camaraderie of work. For others it will be soaring out to new heights on your own. Since femininity is enhanced by masculinity, the intellectual and social exchange with men is a desirable part of life, and it falls in the realm of meaningful friendships which enhance our lives. I think single women can realistically pray for these kinds of male friendships. The quickest way not to realize them is to communicate that you have more in mind than friendship.

No substitute for godliness exists for any woman. God has in mind an abundant life for every believer. If we are not growing it is because we have not handled what God has told us to handle. We can complain about our lot in life and fuss over our lack of understanding and be much like Job. He was only comforted when God showed him who He was. An adequate view of God takes care of lots of foolishness. His command in our lives is permission, not repression. He makes us free to do that which prepares us for joy — that which will bring the greatest happiness to us.

10

Silver Bells and Cockle Shells

How does your garden grow? For years you've been planting ideas, dreams, deeds and attitudes in the soil of your life. The fragrance and fruit of your plantings are now affecting others. I'm talking about your ministry — the nourishment your life gives someone else. Ministry is the expression of what is inside you; it is the outflow of what you are.

Technically, ministry means to serve, help or comfort on behalf of someone else. In Britain the word is used of government agencies designed to help people; e.g., the Ministry of Education. Educational aid is given on behalf of the government. When we use the word ministry in a Christian sense, we carry this same idea. Service, encouragement, comfort given on behalf of someone else, and that Someone is God. Unfortunately, ministry has become a professional, clerical word shut up to the payroll of the church. Rather it is meant to be the overflow of the life of God in a person.

Ministry implies the importance of people. Jesus said that whenever someone gives a cup of water to a thirsty person, feeds the hungry or clothes the naked, it is the same as if it were done to him. That's how important people are to God. When David finally confessed his sin with Bathsheba to God he said his sin had been against God. Why? Not just because David had broken the law, but the law was there in the first place because God made Bathsheba, and her personhood was important to him. The entire Bible spells out the importance of people in God's sight. The two great Commandments tell us to love God with our whole being, and our neighbor as our self. When God fills a life with himself, ministry is a natural fruit.

Let's take a look at your ministry. You may be one of those people who think of ministry in terms of a stirring talk, a magnificent prayer or a beautiful song. A public performance means ministry to you and you say, "I have no ministry." If you really have no ministry, it is not for lack of a talent but because of inner barrenness. The influence of a growing, aware life with God will always be more profound than you know. You may not be shouting, "Look at me ministering" but that's just as well. That kind of ministering leads to pride. It's like having too much sun in your garden; it dries out the roots.

I've always liked Barnabas, whom I met in the book of *The Acts.* His chief ministry seemed to be that of encouraging other people. When others were wary of a converted Paul, Barnabas found him and encouraged him to exercise his ministry. Paul became the outstanding missionary, but Barnabas' encouragement got him going. Later when Paul was disappointed with the instability of John Mark, it was Barnabas who took John Mark as his companion and encouraged him in the ministry.

Encouragement is a spiritual ministry; it is God's ministry to you. He always encourages you. If you feel discouraged you'll find Satan is the source of discouragement. Check out your own garden. Is encouragement one of the strong plants in your life? Encouragement brings out the best in people; it is love taking hold of another hand and placing it in the courage of God.

Every wife ought to be learning how to encourage a discouraged husband. She will do this in numerous ways by sowing seeds of praise, by praying, by her godly perspective, by simply saying, "I'm sticking with you." I don't

mean Pollyanna sunshine talk that doesn't face a real
world. Think of the inner resources it takes to understand
the world your husband faces and to minister encouragement without manipulating his affairs or giving way to
foolish fears. Encouragement is the overflow of the life of
God in you.

A mother has almost a full-time ministry of encouragement. My mother set the tone for our whole day by her
attitude toward us as we awoke each morning. She often
had a song, and always a word of good cheer. The critical,
nagging mother can effectively ruin a whole day before it
begins. It takes a good portion of creativity to encourage
children to be their very best. Hashing over past naughtiness and spouting out negative expectations produces
naughtiness and negative behavior. You get what you expect. Encouragement, on the other hand, can encourage a
child to believe in himself and in God.

And what of encouraging your parents as they grow
older, or your fellow teacher or the neighbor in the next
apartment? Anyone who herself is encouraged by God
can encourage others. That's the secret. In the Old Testament when David was beset by danger from King Saul,
the Scripture reads, "David encouraged himself in the
Lord his God" (1 Samuel 30:6). Then David was in position to encourage others.

The screaming mother in the grocery store, chastising
and humiliating her child with words that have a far
more lasting sting than a spanking, demonstrates the life
that has no inflow of divine resources. Her complaints to
her husband and her rejection of his attention betray the
tragedy of her uptight life. *Encouragement!* Thou art a
flower of magnificent fragrance. Lord, sow such seeds
liberally in our lives.

I have a beautiful friend with five small children. She
is sensitive to each child's needs in an unusual way and
tries to encourage each one where they need it. And her
spirit is catching. I notice that the children encourage each
other because of her encouragement. They were all at the
school program together one night to watch David per-
form. He goofed and missed his cue, and the whole family

suffered with him, knowing how much it meant to him to do well. Afterwards, I heard them as they gathered around David, who bemoaned his error. One sympathized, another mentioned how clearly he spoke his lines — each one thought of something encouraging to say to comfort David, because he was so important to his family.

Anyone who wants a worldwide ministry needs only to learn to pray. Prayer unleashes the activity of God on behalf of those brought before him — and it changes us. It is the most enriching of ministries because it brings us into God's presence. We become like the people with whom we spend time. But prayer is the most neglected of ministries. Too often our humanness wants our ministry to be seen by others. We need visible, immediate response. No one knows how much we pray, except God.

Tragically, many women would rather fuss and feel sorry for themselves than to pray. Prayer can keep a husband on track, realizing the best for his personal life. Prayer can take away a mother's bitterness, can change a father's drunkenness, can alter situations and attitudes, can keep children safe in a strife-filled school. Job prayed for his children, lest they be careless in sinning. Hannah prayed for a godly son. You can pray for a calm heart, a gentle spirit, and for all the sensitive miracles needed in the dynamics of your family life.

The KJV Bible speaks of the *succour* God offers in time of need. Adequate, appropriate help. I was reading Hebrews 2 one day in my Quiet Time and I began questioning what kind of help God would offer. What would the quality of his help be? It came to me forcefully that he would offer only holy help. It would be consistent with his character. Then I saw why I didn't always come to him for the help I needed. If the help offered was holy, then I would have to change. That meant self-pity had to go, attitudes would be changed. Praying invites God to change our situation — and us.

And you can pray beyond your walls. Years ago we were asked to call on a sick woman from our church. We went hoping to be encouraging, and came away twice blessed. The woman was old, bed-ridden, and childless. Her husband in his own feebleness took loving care of her. Essentially both of them were cut off from active participation in the world. Yet next to her bed the husband had devised a pyramid stand that turned on a swivel. The faces of the pyramid were covered with the pictures of missionaries. And when she could not sleep in the night, she turned to her missionaries and prayed for hours for the needs of the world. Together they were remarkably well-informed. From the newspaper, the radio, the television and letters they kept abreast of what was happening. They prayed for kings and governments, for councils and mayors, for school superintendents and police chiefs.

One day when we stopped to see her, she was almost ecstatic with joy. She had heard a man speak over the radio and felt that doctrinally he lacked sound teaching. She had no way to get to him, except to pray that God would somehow show him his error. The doorbell had rung that afternoon, and the radio speaker stood on the doorstep as a visitor. He had heard of this remarkable bed-ridden lady through a friend and felt he should call. He was as pleased as she when she shared the story of her concern. That dear lady did not physically leave her house for years, and yet families, individuals, society itself felt the impact of her ministry, and some of them were prayed to her front door.

Jesus said, "Men ought always to pray and not to faint." We live in a day when the heart of people fails for fear. Tensions in the school. The breakdown of moral codes. Increase in crime. Why not have a ministry of praying, instead of complaining!

In many ways it is easier to pray with someone than alone. Your spiritual life and ministry will grow if you find a compatible prayer-partner. It's something to ask God for. Meeting regularly to pray with a friend for your personal needs and hers will provoke the kind of honest sharing that will bring you both closer to the Lord. You will be simply astounded at what will happen as you talk to God together.

Recently a woman shared with me her concern for a daughter who was rebellious and operating in open warfare against her parents. We talked about some possible causes that might be eliminated, because practical objective wisdom is part of our ministry to others. But then I asked if she and her husband, both of whom claimed to know God, could spend fifteen minutes every evening praying for their daughter. Her eyes dropped, she hesitated and was reluctant. Her attitude showed where some of the problems was. I suggested she begin praying that they could pray!

A quiet ministry comes from what we are. God is always more concerned about what we are than what we do. And if we are self-centered and shallow, petty and critical, then we need to pull handfuls of weeds from the garden so some other plants can flourish. God's promises are not to the slothful and negligent. He expects us to *become.* There are women who minister unconsciously to others out of a wealth of good thinking. They make it their business to read the right books, to appreciate what is worthwhile, while at the same time living with the problems of a real world. In other words, they have it put together. Life, that is.

Married women are especially privileged to have the luxury to be this kind of person. Too few appreciate or realize the potential of their opportunities. They can "nourish their souls with good works, give it peace in solitude, get it strength in prayer, make it wise with reading, enlighten it by meditation, make it tender with love, sweeten it with psalms and hymns, and comfort it with frequent reflections upon future glory!"[1]

What? You say, I have four children. Ten years of great effort, maybe even twenty. But still more luxury to meditate and love and sing and reflect — and even read and have some solitude — than anyone else. And after the ten or twenty years the pattern will already be set in motion. You will have even more time — time to paint, to write, to garden, to take up a new hobby, to run for Congress — and to continue to do good works. You will be forever what you are becoming today.

[1] William Law, *A Serious Call to a Devout and Holy Life,* p. 38.

Obviously gifts vary greatly in the exercising of ministry. The Bible speaks of this realistically, and says that in the body the greater parts cannot say they do not need the lesser parts. It is only as everyone ministers that the needs of the whole body are met. The challenge in exercising a gift in the ministry is to do for others rather than for self-gratification. The musician who wants to minister to others will keep the needs of her audience in mind. Otherwise she may show excellent voice control and a marvelous range, but there will be no ministry. Teachers do not teach subjects, they teach people, if they want to minister. Homemakers make a home for people, not for the sake of perfection. Good cooks prepare food for enjoyment, not for praise.

I think of a diligent woman who volunteered to be in charge of the visual aid materials for a small school. She wanted a ministry. She became obsessed with the perfection of the materials and their arrangement. She worked very hard, and did an excellent job. But she became possessive. Procedures for the use of materials became so complicated that people stopped using them. She had a perfect department with no ministry. People are the point of any ministry, and we do well to remind ourselves of this.

Serving others ought to help us reach outside our own homes and families. We begin at home. Those who cannot minister to the people who are closest to them are unwilling to face the basic relationships of life. Their motivation is self-gratification, not ministry. It's not uncommon to find a woman who will involve herself deeply in a counseling ministry with others but won't listen to her own mother for more than five minutes. She is expansive with understanding for the stranger, but critical of her own family.

There are many ways to hide from outreach to others. The married woman can hide behind her children and use them as an excuse for lack of involvement in the world. The single woman can hide behind her career and her fatigue, increasingly living an in-grown life. But neither of these may realize what they are doing.

I was so pleased when Alice moved into her own apartment. Now she could invite some of her single teacher friends home for a meal and hopefully a meaningful conversation. She had a place where she could initiate a Bible study. I knew some of the people with whom she taught, and several were hurting inside and needed some love and understanding. But Alice didn't respond to either her apartment or God that way. Her concept of stewardship of possessions was nil, and she grew increasingly content to schedule her life around her new color television set. It was not until she went to a conference where a speaker honed in on the Lordship of Christ that the veil came from before her eyes.

Opportunities to minister are thousand-fold. The neighborhood Bible study, or the study in the office. A good lending library, with enthusiasm for books. Transporting and working with handicapped children in a special program. Volunteer work at a hospital. Remembering to bring something small, but beautiful to a friend. Just plain thoughtfulness. Listening to others. Teaching a Sunday school class. Leading a study group. Helping in the kitchen.

I read recently about a Mrs. Ethel Miller in Washington State who heard of the need for surgical tools in mission hospitals. She began to wonder if doctors didn't collect more tools than they needed, just as she did in her kitchen. She called two doctors she knew, and they both had equipment they willingly donated. It began with a small project to help one mission hospital. Today she and a group of retired people ship enormous quantities of drug samples and surgical supplies to Africa and Asia. She's been doing this for seventeen years, since the day she first said "yes" to God when he prompted the idea.

Thus far, the discussion on ministry has centered on our personal good works and the ministries of our conduct. This has been deliberate. We are whole people, and we need to see that ministry comes out of what we are. Now it's time to talk about our verbal witness to God's grace. In sharing the good news of salvation we are often tempted to pour truth over another's head. I have heard the phrase, "I gave her a witness," and wondered what that meant. Did it mean that she said something religious or gave a Scripture verse or what? How we live must support our words. We cannot avoid the discipline of having God work out his beauty in our lives, and when we share Jesus Christ with someone else it is in the context of this discipline.

The really Christian home is a great boon to sharing our faith. It is like a city set on a hill which cannot be hid. In any neighborhood when others observe a family trusting God, forgiving each other, affirming each other as people, living together in loving relationship, they take a second look: What does this family have? They see a "redemptive society" within the family, reflecting the reality of the Christian message.

The same thing takes place wherever people are truly Christian in their behavior patterns. Thoughtfulness, encouragement, helpfulness, a loving attitude — these all create a natural climate in which to share faith.

And if what you believe means anything at all to you, you will find yourself speaking about it to others. You must speak. No one finds life in Christ simply by admiring the way you live. They must believe in Christ personally. Many non-Christians have healthy, whole ways to live, and unless you talk about your faith no one will be able to tell the difference.

Someone has defined sharing your faith as "one beggar telling another beggar where to find bread." I like that because it underscores the necessity for humility in evangelism. A redeemed sinner speaks, not a religious superior. If you "blow it" you can ask to be forgiven! Secondly, it emphasizes the need. People are lost, hungry, empty, dead in their sins without God. Some of them feel uneasy because they already suspect this is true; others have not begun to define their need. Having experienced what it means to be forgiven, to be made a member of God's family, you've got good news to share. You know what they need to know.

This necessitates your understanding the big picture of what the Gospel really is all about. You want to communicate the heart of the message, without cultural trimmings, in a way that makes sense. And it does make sense. Man feels alienated from God. He can either try to rationalize why this is so, or he can come to terms with the holiness of God, the sinfulness of man, the meaning of the death of Christ, and what it means to live a Christian life under the Lordship of Christ. But people have to hear the message in order to believe.

Hearing can come in a variety of settings. You can invite someone to church, but that is less personal and can make the person feel self-consciousness. Someone may ask, "What do you believe?" Which gives you a free opportunity to share. But more often we need to take time, to invest ourselves in communication which maximizes the person's opportunity to understand. Learn to ask questions. Jesus did this all the time. A good question can set in motion a whole process of understanding the inadequacy of unbelief and the sensibility of belief. If you are alert, you will find the conversation of every day affords many opportunities for such questions or the remark which provokes a further query from your friend. We need to learn how to relax, be honest and speak openly. The natural witness is more effective than the contrived, and we are not in this alone. God cares about other people far more than we do. He has invested the life of his Son in their redemption. He simply asks us to share the message.

Small group Bible studies provide a natural setting for learning and sharing together. Three or four — and certainly no more than ten — discussing a passage of Scripture can be like dynamite in individual lives. Ask, don't tell. Use a good discussion guide that insists that you go back to the biblical text to discover what it is saying. Groups like these in neighborhods, in schools, in offices and in homes are changing people. And those involved are experiencing the joy of sharing their own faith. This works for the married, the single, teenagers — wherever people are prepared to think.

The potential for our ministry is the potential found in the heart of a creative God. We need to say, "May I?" to God, not "Must I?" And if our will is set on reaching out, our faith will take us beyond the obstacles or difficulties we see. The willing heart, the full to overflowing heart — the possessors of these have an influence all out of proportion to their person. How pathetic to come in close contact with many lives and to have made no notable difference to others. Influencing others is inevitable when we have furnished our spirits with good things.

My favorite poet, Luci Shaw, expresses my own heart in her poem *Hundredfold.*

> Yesterday
> (after first frost, with maples
> blazing beyond fringes of stubble hay)
> my husband and my sons
> pulled up dead summer's stalks of corn
> laying them flat among the weeds
> for plowing in again when next spring's born.
>
> I'm glad I picked the green tomatoes
> two nights ago
> and spread them, newspapered
> to ripen on the basement floor
> good company for the corn relish, row
> and golden row in jars behind the closet door.
>
> Yes, I'm very glad
> something's left — something not dead
> after all the hilling and hoeing
> seeding and sprouting, greening and growing —
> after the blowing
> tassels high as a woman's hand above her head
>
> > *Corn relish for Sunday dinner — grace*
> > *the days when outside snowings*
> > *whiten winter's face!*
>
> Let me leave fruit
> (but not in someone's basement)
> when I grow browned
> and old and pulled up by the root
> and laid down flat
> and ploughed into the ground.[2]

---

[2] Reprinted from *Listen to the Green,* by Luci Shaw, Harold Shaw Publishers, Wheaton, Illinois. Used by permission.

11

Shape Up

Every woman is packaged differently. You can generally find a packaging you like better than yours, but happily you will always find some that make you thankful for your own. Sizes and shapes differ physically, yes — but emotionally, intellectually and temperamentally the packaging varies, too. And that variety is both the spice and trouble of life.

Some women have managed to shape up and ship out into the mainstream of life, handling the currents and the rapids and the quiet pools with a gracious, confident ease. Others are trapped in one eddy after another, going nowhere at all, hung up in swirling pockets of confusion. Everyone gets sidetracked once in a while, and requires a rescue operation. That's the way life is. But some have been caught in an eddy or on a piece of dead wood for so long that they have forgotten that life was meant to be lived in the mainstream.

Too many people are weighted down with appendages and loads they were never meant to carry. We are our own worst enemies. We harbor the ugly and neglect the good. Too early we lie down under the burden and say, "That's just the way I am." *I am so foolish. I am good-for-nothing. I am full of fears. I am so bad-tempered. I am weak in this area. I am jealous.* Our lives are full of wretched *I ams* that spell failure. The *I am* that can rescue us is the *I AM* of God. He says, *I am the all-sufficient One.* Remember when the people of Israel, in bondage to Egypt, asked Moses the name of the one who would deliver them. God said, "Tell them *I AM* has sent you." God's name is *I AM* and behind that *I AM* are all the resources we need. He says, "I am your peace. I am your strength. I am your deliverance." His *I AM* cancels out our failures.

Below is a list of words which describe different kinds of women. Look it over carefully. Check off the combinations which describe you.

> Scared and frigid
> Nervous and demanding
> Warm and loving
> Callous and thoughtless
> Boisterous and nervy
> Pessimistic and small-minded
> Gabby and short-tempered
> Sensitive and self-conscious
> Always right and misunderstood
> Perfectionist and rigid
> Wise and understanding
> Sensual and undisciplined
> Complaining and unthankful
> Jealous and possessive
> Thoughtful and appreciative
> Fearful and uncertain

Which of these burdensome realities would you like to unload?

You can be different. That is one of the joys of knowing God. We are not stuck with what we are. Many of us are like the woman who was walking to the market in town carrying a heavy load on her back. A friend came past in a wagon and offered her a ride. The woman thankfully climbed aboard, but still sat there bowed under the weight of the burden. Finally her friend said, "Why don't you put your load down on the floor of the wagon?"

The woman replied, "It's very good of you to take me to town. I couldn't ask you to carry my burden, too." We need God for disasters, for the final moment of death, but isn't it asking a lot of him to help us get rid of our measly, uncomfortable burdens?

I am reminded of a story that Corrie Ten Boom tells of a journey she took into Amsterdam with her father as a small girl. Her father had purchased a suitcase full of parts for his watchmaking business and when the train was nearing their home station, he asked Corrie if she would like to carry the suitcase off the train. She was eager to try, but could move it scarcely an inch. Then her father wisely said, "Remember, Corrie, there are some things too heavy for you to carry. You must give them to your heavenly Father, just as you must let me carry this case off the train." In the years that followed when Corrie was interned by the Germans in a concentration camp during World War II those words came back to her often, and she would pray, "Father, this is too heavy for me to carry. I will give it to you."

But the starting point is admitting to the symptoms that make our lives diseased. Dis-eased, that is. Some may be overly sensitive and wondered if they didn't have all the negative traits on the list. Others read it over and checked off only the positives or else skipped over it completely. Why the difference? The first case could be a low self-concept or an overly eager attempt to be honest. The second could be self-protection or an inability even to evaluate one's own person.

This is why it is so important to have daily fellowship with God where your spirit is tuned in to listen as you read the Bible and pray. God is a good teacher. He points out one thing at a time for us to work on. When we feel like a confused failure, that too much needs to be changed all at once, then the source of our feelings is not God, but our enemy. God will help us deal with one item at a time. He puts a gentle finger on first one thing and then another and suddenly we have insights into ourselves that we never had before. The person who never has a new insight either has no hang-ups — or she isn't listening!

Look back over the descriptive list of personality types. How many of these could be taken care of if you simply *believed* God loved you? Believing this would give you a different self-concept and potentially free you from many habits. But it isn't a push-button cure. You believe and then you must take a stand repeatedly on what you believe. Thoughts come to you, and you resist them and say. "I will not feel that way because I know. . . ."

A second question. Looking back over the list, how many of these *might* be eliminated if your physical condition were different? Some of these traits are possibly most conspicuous at the time of the month which corresponds to the monthly menstrual cycle. Or maybe the thyroid is out of whack. Or you are suffering from anemia or some other malfunction. I learned long ago to inquire into people's physical health in dealing with spiritual problems. One affects the other, and it works both ways. Fearfulness, uncertainty, sensitivity, nervousness can cause physical problems. In that event the solution is a spiritual one. On the other hand, a run-down physical condition can cause spiritual problems. Some people need to see a medical doctor and take some hormones or an iron pill. Others need the discipline of more sleep and a slower pace.

A third question: How many of these traits stem from just plain old-fashioned sinfulness? Self-centeredness is the cause of at least half of these traits. It's the opposite of being filled with the love of God. Any time we are more conscious of ourselves than we are of others or of God, we are in a trap, an eddy that keeps us out of the mainstream of life as it ought to be lived.

What's the solution? It is found in the Beatitudes. We begin by recognizing spiritual poverty. *Blessed are the poor in spirit.* We mourn because we are so poor in spirit. *Blessed are they that mourn for they shall be comforted.* We realize that in ourselves we cannot become what we need to be; we need God's love to fill us. *Blessed are the meek.* We hunger and thirst for God himself. *Blessed are those who hunger and thirst for righteousness for they shall be satisfied.* Hungering and thirsting for God changes our whole set of priorities, our viewpoint, our life style. God fills our hearts with his love when we are hungry to know him. We are changed by a spiritual exercise born out of intense desire to be rid of a most disfiguring burden — self-centeredness.

It hurts to face your sins. Admitting that you lose your temper or get angry is hard on the ego. If you mean business about cleaning up your life, you'll have to learn how to ask for forgiveness and say, "I'm sorry" to others — your husband, your children, your mother-in-law, your friends. If you are *really* sorry for your lack of control, you'll stop rationalizing about what caused it and how you couldn't help yourself and earnestly ask God to quiet your insides and work out patience in your daily experience. And you'll learn that at the moment when the flare-up is being ignited you can turn instantaneously to God for strength and control. "O Lord, calm me down. Give me your perspective. Fill me with your love." And he will.

We can't forget the woman who gets a great psychological boost from telling someone off, and then recounting her cleverness in lengthy descriptions to others. *I really told her,* she says. It may be a business deal, a child's teacher, a fellow employee, but whoever or whatever, the abrasiveness of the situation makes the rest of the world cringe. Some people collect resentments and outrages. I think of the Lord Jesus who *was* right and righteous, and how people marveled at the gracious words he spoke. When the boisterous, the aggressively nervy, the always-right, the bellicose come into his presence they must hang their heads. God wants to provide amply for inner needs that cause us to act in these ways. He wants to take care of our need to feel superior by making us like Jesus Christ.

Some people are angry at God. Perfectionists often are, even though they won't admit it. Life hasn't been neat and tidy and the way they planned! Anger at God is a symptom. The basic problem is unbelief. God isn't in charge, or if he is, he blew it. Which says not so much about God as about them. Perfectionists want to be God's chief counselors because they don't believe he can do it without them.

Unbelief is the most disastrous of all our attitudes. It keeps us from coming to God for the resources we need.

We don't believe he can produce the goods! We are not sure he is completely trustworthy and so we try to limp along pretending a faith we haven't realized. Unbelief makes people sick mentally, physically and emotionally. A painful lot of the mental and emotional uncertainties experienced by so many could be solved best by learning how to believe and how to cast one's self on the goodness of God.

The biggest burden carried around is the load of guilt. It drags us down with a steady pull. For how many people does a simple theft return again and again to haunt and destroy inner peace! I recently heard someone tell how she had knowingly accepted two one dollar bills stuck together when she had only been entitled to the payment of one. For twenty years she had felt unclean over that incident. Whenever she came close to God, this miserable memory made a barrier. Finally with the encouragement of God through reading the Bible she decided to be done with it once for all. She first confessed the sin to God and asked forgiveness, and then she wrote a letter, returning the dollar bill with an explanation. It was only a dollar bill, you say. No, it was a theft, and what a costly load it made. Twenty years of guilt that was unnecessary.

Restitution cannot always be made for mistakes we make, but where it is sensible it should be done, simply because it is right. And it is a therapeutic purging. However, if our attempt to make restitution causes more hurt than help, it can be the selfish therapy of unbelief that makes our actions more important than God's. When God has forgiven us, then what is crucial has been done. This is especially true in the area of sexual sins where some women feel constrained to confess all when the end result is only further hurt, not healing. God's forgiveness is enough in instances like these. And if no one else is involved in our wrong-doing, then the one to tell is God, not the whole world.

Do you know the quality of God's forgiveness? The Bible says, "As far as the east is from the west, so far does he remove our transgressions from us" (Psalm 103:12). "I, I am He who blots out your transgressions for my own sake, and I will not remember your sins" (Isaiah 43:25). "I have swept away your transgressions like a cloud, and your sins like mist; return to me, for I have redeemed you" (Isaiah 44:22). "If we confess our sins, he is faithful and just, and will forgive our sins and cleanse us from all unrighteousness" (1 John 1:9). He removes our sins; he blots them out; he will not remember them; he sweeps them away; he cleanses us from *all* unrighteousness. Why would anyone hang onto sins when such provision is made for their disposal?

People cripple themselves with both the memory of wrong deeds done or deeds done against them. God offers to dispose of all our guilt and wipe clean our memories. He offers forgiveness. When we accept it, we are suddenly more free than we have ever been to forgive someone else.

Is there any kind of sin he will not forgive? None, except the ultimate refusal to come to him, which denies the Holy Spirit's ministry to us. People worry about the unpardonable sin instead of coming to him to be pardoned. Some would make sex sins the next thing to unpardonable, but God lists them along with gossiping and coveting. The Bible says that sex sins have serious consequences because they are sins against our own bodies and affect another's body as well. But no one needs wear a scarlet letter *A* and be so presumptuous as to think they can make atonement for their own sins. Christ died for our sins. He invites us to confess our sins and be forgiven. Healthy people are forgiven people and forgiving people.

I emphasize this because many people enjoy wallowing around in the past, reviewing their sins and almost revelling in the sorrow of their guilt. Others forget everything else except the sins of others. Spiritual health is forgetting what is behind and pressing on to the mark of the high call of God in Jesus Christ.

Some sins become habits, like lying. Isaiah the prophet wrote about this long ago. He said, "We have made lies our refuge, and in falsehood we have taken shelter" (Isaiah 28:15b). The liar has a quarrel with life; it isn't good enough as it is. Lying thus reflects on the character

of God. People lie because of low self-esteem, to get attention, to take advantage of someone else, to destroy
them, and for a variety of other unfortunate reasons. Lying
makes no sense because it usually hurts the liar most. But
that is characteristic of sin. Lying means you have to keep
your lies straight, which seems a terrible trouble unless
you live in an unreal world. Jesus called the devil the
father of lies.

The best way to beat the lying habit is to confess your
lies to the people to whom you have lied and ask their
forgiveness. Nothing is harder on pride, and if you mean
business with God he will help you break out of this trap
by facing the consequences of lying. Then if you ask him
he will be your constant, present help to keep you from
repeating the habit.

Confession to others helps break any habit, because it
asks for human support in your weakness. If the habit is
a private one, the encouragement of one loyal friend who
has the integrity to help you may be a tremendous boon.
For example, confessing our fears to such a friend gets
them out in the open where they can be looked at honestly. Most of us think no one else ever feels as we do,
and we are surprised to discover that others really understand. And sometimes when things are out in the open
they seem less serious than we thought in private. Another
person can hold us to our intentions and help us break
habits as well.

Jealousy is one fear that prompts a lot of foolish behavior.
Some jealousy is petty and stupid; *she spoke to her first,
not to me* or *their son was chosen last time* kind of thing.
Or the second wife who is jealous of a father's love for his
children and does all she can to drive them apart, thus
managing to make a loveless home. Some mothers can't
let their children belong to anyone else at marriage, and
some children can't let their parents re-marry. The Bible
calls jealousy coveteousness, which is the same as idolatry.
It's a matter of worshiping at the wrong shrine again.

Other jealousy comes from deeper hurts: a husband who
flirts or whose business is suspiciously monkey business.
God knows how unfaithfulness hurts, so go to him and get

your strength and comfort there. Your hurt is best kept a private affair, and if you are wise, you'll take an inventory to see whether anything in your life has made it easier for your husband even to think unfaithful thoughts. Obviously no one is perfect, but we can be too busy, too tired to love, too unconcerned with his world, too careless in our appearance — and make the temptation of someone who isn't too tired or too busy more appealing.

Here is where your prayer life will prove the power of God. In fact, if your life together is lived in the Lord's presence with integrity, and if you are praying honestly together with each other, unfaithfulness is an unlikely event. And especially if your husband does not share your personal faith in God, your prayers for him will keep him and bless him in ways he will never understand. But a careful life must back up your prayers.

No matter how we rationalize in the end, jealousy turns out to be a manifestation of unbelief. It is the opposite of a faith point of view. It must go to the rubbish heap with the rest of the trapping we collect that keep us from really living life.

Feeling neglected you may have some temptations yourself. It's a free-swinging world that says only happiness counts, that if it makes you happy then it is good. Nonsense. Our lives must reflect the character of God if they are to know anything about the real stuff of happiness. *Happy are those who hunger and thirst after righteousness for they are satisfied.* And it is of inestimable worth to grow old liking yourself and having no regrets.

A word about temptation, any temptation — the temptation to swear, drink, be angry, sleep too much, lie or shout at your children. God has made provision for every kind of temptation. "No temptation has overtaken you that is not common to man. God is faithful, and he will not let you be tempted beyond your strength, but with the temptation will also provide the way of escape, that you may be able to endure it" (1 Corinthians 10:13). That is one important verse in the Bible. Others before you have been tempted as you are. No one needs to be swept away as a helpless victim. Claim this promise and memorize it.

We've scarcely scratched the surface of all our hang-ups and touchy places that need to be discarded and cleaned up if we are to live life as it is meant to be lived. Paul wrote a good word to the Ephesians when he said, *Live life, then, with a due sense of responsibility, not as those who do not know the meaning and purpose of life, but as those who do. Make the best use of your time, despite all the difficulties of these days. Don't be vague, but firmly grasp what you know to be the will of God.*[1]

---

[1] Ephesians 5:15 (Phillips)

12

Freedom

One misty cold Sunday morning in the northwoods she came into my life as a visitor from a nearby resort. Her name was Lisa, a Vassar student, and she had recently met the first real Christians she had ever known. They told her about our camping program for university students, and so she had come. It was time for morning worship, and I invited her into the lodge for the service.

She took in the student participation with relaxed and casual interest. But as the speaker began to read she strained forward as if to drink in every phrase. He read, "But the fruit of the Spirit is

> love
> joy
> peace
> patience
> kindness
> goodness
> faithfulness
> gentleness
> self-control . . ."

He let each quality drop as a gem to be admired as he read. As quickly as the list was finished she turned to me with brimming eyes, gripped my arm and said in a loud whisper, "That's what it is. That's what makes them so special!"

Looking at that cluster of fruit she thought, not of abstract ideas, but of two people. Those words described the Christians she had met. And the compelling quality of their lives made Lisa eager to know the source of such inner beauty. Small wonder she had said of them, "They are nice to know!"

The fruit of the Spirit never looked more winsome then during my talk with Lisa. Since then I have turned many times to Galatians 5, to read these verses in their context. The chapter begins: *For freedom Christ has set us free; stand fast therefore, and do not submit again to a yoke of slavery.* The subject is freedom. Christ has set us free — free to have this kind of fruit in our lives. Love. Joy. Peace. Patience. Kindness. Goodness. Faithfulness. Gentleness. Self-control.

That is freedom worth talking about. Not just a freedom to talk about, but a freedom to experience, to have worked out at the core of life. Not an abstract idea, but a reality which others can identify.

What is this freedom Christ offers? It is the freedom of acceptance with God. No one has to work his way to the divine; God comes himself to take away our guilt and graciously call us to himself. Upon our individual response to him, we are released from slavery and made his dear children, given all the family privileges.

Why would anyone experiencing such freedom from bondage be warned against submitting again to a yoke of slavery? It does seem absurd. But so easily we take back the management of our own affairs. We stop believing; we stop obeying. Our humanness gets in the way and pulls our eyes from God's supply to our own resources. We begin filling our own needs. Somehow, we believe we have to be good enough to make it to God. We've accepted his standard now, which makes performance even harder. Bondage.

Falling away from freedom into bondage is one problem. The Bible mentions another. It talks about freedom which leads to license. We're forgiven; we're accepted. We're free, aren't we? Let's do our own thing. The Bible calls this "using your freedom as an opportunity for the flesh" — freedom as a launching pad for selfishness. How quickly freedom can fall into the pit of selfishness; distorted and twisted, bearing no likeness to the freedom to which we've been called.

The freedom Christ has given us is the freedom to reach our highest potential. Paul wrote earlier in this Galatian letter of his longing "that Christ be formed in you!" or "until you take the shape of Christ" (NEB). That is our potential. And we are not passive participants in this likeness to Christ.

The battleground is within us. Freedom is ours; but slavery is also a choice. Paul says, "Walk by the Spirit and do not gratify the desires of the flesh. For the desires of the flesh are against the Spirit, and the desires of the Spirit are against the flesh; for these are opposed to each other, to prevent you from doing what you would" (Galatians 5:16, 17). He is talking about a realistic inner conflict. Christians possess two natures. The flesh is what we are by natural birth; the Spirit is the Holy Spirit who causes us to be "born again," to come alive spiritually. He is the One who indwells us. These two, the flesh and the Spirit, oppose each other in what has been called an "irreconcilable antagonism." Certainly as we learn to "walk by the Spirit" our old nature is increasingly subdued, but this comes by daily commitment, through daily right choices.

What is the choice I must make? I must decide who will direct my life — my old nature or the Holy Spirit. It is not self-effort that keeps us on track, but the Holy Spirit. It is yielding to him. Without him we end up with the *works of the flesh,* instead of the *fruit of the Spirit. Works vs. fruit.* The fruit comes from having our roots deep into the refreshment of God. He produces the fruit.

In contrast, the works of the flesh are obvious (Galatians 5:19-21): "Fornication, impurity and indecency; idolatry and sorcery; quarrels, a contentious temper, envy, fits of rage, selfish ambitions, dissensions, party intrigues,

and jealousies; drinking bouts, orgies, and the like."
(NEB)

Contrasting *the works* and *the fruit* ought to sufficiently
discipline our lives. Who would choose *works* to *fruit*?
Yet there are some people whose lives are a constant round
of ups and downs. Defeat and victory, depending on who
is in control. The Bible says there is only one way to handle the problem. *Those who belong to Christ Jesus have
crucified the flesh with its passions and desires* (Galatians 5:24).

Crucified is a no half measure. It is pitiless and painful.
It is decisive action. We nail our hang-ups to the cross,
our poor, base desires which get us in trouble, and we
leave them there. John Stott amplifies the significance of
this by pointing out that death by crucifixion is not sudden, but gradual. While our old desires may often rear
their heads, they have been nailed to the cross and we
are determined to keep them there until they die.[1]

The great secret of the Christian life is the decisiveness
of our intention. Some people never intend to obey the
Gospl by submitting to the Lord. They try to arrange life
so they can admit to the truth of Christianity without giving up themselves. They come again and again for coun-
sel, for forgiveness; they may seek out psychiatrists or
medical doctors for woes of the mind and flesh caused by
their inability to give up. They need to decide to obey
God by letting the Spirit control their lives.

You can think of a dozen illustrations from your own
life, and so can I. Amy, for instance, had a problem with
drugs. She started out "cool," just wanting a bit of a lift
for her spirits, and ended up flat out and suicidal. She
was invited to come to God for help and forgiveness. She
struggled and kicked all the way and eventually went
through the motion of giving her life to Christ. Her con-
version seemed genuine, but as time went on she took out
all her "works of the flesh" and handled them again to
see if they were dead. They weren't. Her ups were less
frequent than her downs. She was fitful, restless. Clearly

---

[1] John R. W. Stott, *The Message of Galatians,* Inter-Varsity
Press.

she was not letting the Spirit direct her life. A confrontation was essential. Was she serious or not in her intent to give her life to Christ?

Only God knows when she really became his own child, but it was not until she abandoned herself to God that she began to develop the inner decisiveness to make choices that led to walking by the Spirit. Amy had never really given up her secret love for the weakness of her flesh. Drugs and sex still were an alive appeal that needed to be crucified. She could not crucify them by herself. When she gave herself completely, nothing held back, God captured her affection and gave her the help she needed.

The Spirit-controlled life is no faky role-playing. One person may have a well-developed personality, good digestion, and enough savvy to know how to live with others and thus be quite pleasant company. Another may grit his teeth and try to produce synthetic love and joy, in spite of poor digestion and many conflicts, in order to get along with others. Some may even enroll in charm courses hoping to become fascinating women. Others learn how to manage situations psychologically, taking apart the components of actions and conversations for analysis — and so managing life.

But this is self-effort, not the work of the Spirit in a person. In daily situations we have two choices: to handle it on our own, or to let the Spirit direct us. As we choose the latter, he works out a cluster of fruit in our life. I mention a cluster because the Bible doesn't say *fruits,* it says *fruit.* It's all of one piece. I can't say, Lord, I'll have a lot of love and joy, but forget about the faithfulness and self-control. Or I like apples and pears, but forget about plums. It is not *fruits,* but *fruit.* Each is attached to the other. It's the total picture of godly character.

Each characteristic mentioned reflects the character of God himself. *Love, joy, peace.* He is the source of each, and it is his activity in our lives which produces genuine love, genuine joy, and genuine peace. Wouldn't you like to hang a sign on your door reading, "LOVE, JOY, PEACE LIVE HERE"? What a beautiful trio to have

embodied in a person! We've already discussed God's kind
of love and the meaning of joy in other chapters. But
peace alone could fill a book. Peace with God. The peace
of God. Peace: possession of adequate resources. Peace:
the absence of conflict. Peace comes from what we know
about God, not from what we know about ourselves.
Shalom is a Hebrew greeting. Did this originate with
God's activity in revealing himself and his plan of
redemption?

Every household should have the quality of *Shalom*. It
makes home a safe place. But it must come from your
own heart as the tangible part of the fruit of the Spirit.
Peace is not just an abstract ideal; it is a valid experience.
Children are touched by peace, and so is everyone else.
A boy once remarked about his mother, "She makes me
quieter inside."

Patience is another translation for longsuffering. It
means steady under pressure. How patient God is with
us! I remember a woman taking me to lunch one day
and asking, "If Gerald doesn't change by the end of the
year, don't you think it would be okay for me to go ahead
and get a divorce?" No one had ever asked me that question before and it left me a bit speechless. But then God
provided the answer in my mind, "I think you can be as
hard on Gerald as God has been on you." Longsuffering.
God knows what that is about. It is inherent to his nature.
He gives mercy upon mercy.

How many times has a woman thrown herself across the
bed and cried out, "God, I can't take it any more. It's too
much!" And God has come with a fresh supply of patience
to cope with a hyperkinetic child, a drinking husband, a
poor job situation, a physical weakness — or whatever your
lot is. Longsuffering or patience isn't always what we
want, but it is what we need from God, from others and
for our own character. God says that his patience and
forbearance is meant to lead men to repentance. Will not
he use our longsuffering to that end as well?

And what can be said of *kindness* and *goodness*? When
we see these in action we appreciate afresh what it means

to be human and made in the image of God. Our need and our aspirations are bound into one.

Faithfulness deserves a whole chapter in a day when vows are easily broken and the whimsy of our hearts leads us to rationalize our inconstancy. Faithfulness reflects God's heart. All of his character is in perfect harmony. We do not have to wonder if today he will be the same as he was yesterday. Will he keep his promise today? Yes. God is faithful.

He wants his children to be like him. That is why he gave so many instructions about paying a vow, about "swearing to your own hurt and changing not." Did you say you would go? Then go. Did you say you would do it? Then do it. Faithfulness means that you can count on a person's integrity. She will not change when she has given her word.

Faithfulness is so rare today that it may become the Spirit's most convincing characteristic in our lives. Look at the ten commandments and observe how many are related to faithfulness — faithfulness in relationships, faithfulness in concern, faithfulness to God.

Some time ago a woman very dear to me left her husband, assuring me that God had told her this was all right because it had been a mistake in the first place. She felt nothing for him at this time. No unsolvable problems marred their marriage. She just preferred life without him. She *felt* a certain way. I protested on the basis of the character of God. What could she find in him which would allow her to be so faithless? She would not talk about God's character or her responsibility. She talked about how she *felt*. The fruit of the spirit is faithfulness — based on a commitment, based on righteousness, based on the character of God. We cannot claim to walk in the Spirit and be unfaithful.

The Spirit will keep us faithful, and because his fruit is one piece, he will fill us with love, joy, peace, patience, kindness, goodness. Faithfulness will not mean barrenness! It will mean godliness.

Gentleness. In a brusque world, what a lovely gem. No

arrogance, no guile in gentleness. The gentle person hears a voice outside herself, and sees a person through the eyes of the Creator. Gentleness forgets self because of concern for others.

Self-control. I listened to an angry woman who couldn't find her off-switch, and thus went on and on, raising her blood pressure and irritating everyone else's gastric juices. Such a small stupid thing set her off. I wondered if she could be that angry over genuine injustice and evil!

I talked to a young woman, newly married, who had trouble doing anything unpleasant because she had never in her life had to do what she didn't want to do. She couldn't discipline her life to have any order. She was always behind mountains of work undone, agreed upon responsibilities which were not completed. Before her sexual attractiveness had made the man in her life over-look things that her best girl friends could have warned him about, but now he was no longer moved by her co-quettish behavior. How do you make yourself do what you don't want to do? she asked. Do it with God's help. The fruit of the Spirit is self-control.

When things don't go right, when they go unexpectedly very wrong: self-control. It's bigger than biting your tongue, or learning to cool it. It is the Spirit's inner-work-ing of peace inside you. Self-control is the opposite of circumstance-control.

Dr. Donald Grey Barnhouse put it this way. "Love is the key. Joy is love singing. Peace is love resting. Long-suffering is love enduring. Kindness is love's touch. Good-ness is love's character. Faithfulness is love's habit. Gentle-ness is love's self-forgetfulness. Self-control is love holding the reins." And if we go on to say that God is love, then we have tied the cord of God's character around this cluster of fruit.

Increasingly as I read this list of the fruit of the Spirit, I long to have this worked out in my daily life. It is the heart of being a Christian woman. The resources of God are available to live this kind of a life, but we are slow to take them. It's hard to keep within a budget. We overspend in almost every area of life except this one. If we believe, says Bishop Houghton, why do we live so far below our spiritual income?

Let me suggest two poor attitudes that cause spiritual paralysis and keep us from moving on with God. 1) We may have unrealistic expectations that defeat us before we even begin. Being human gives us an in-built tendency to blame others for their imperfections and the distress this causes us. We keep waiting for things to change, so we can begin to grow spiritually. Sometimes we try a self-improvement course because we blame ourselves for everything that has gone wrong, and we want to get ourselves in shape to begin to trust God.

The world isn't perfect; our family isn't perfect; our friends aren't perfect, we aren't perfect. None of this takes God by surprise. Why it should surprise sinners that they are imperfect is a mystery. But some women can't believe that God has done much until the situation becomes absolute perfection — which it hardly ever does on earth. For instance, a mother can keep peace from flowing through her home while she waits for everyone to shape up. I know of a woman who fussed because her husband stopped at the tavern every night on his way home from work. When he stopped doing that she fussed because he didn't come to the table at her first call for supper. She forgot all about thanking God that the tavern was no longer an issue.

Another woman I know prayed that God would help her daughter become a better student at school. When the daughter's attitude changed and she moved up to a *C* average, the mother kept pushing and praying that she would become an *A* student. Kathleen was not made to be an *A* student; she was a loving, kind *C* student. Her mother had unrealistic goals based on her view of how things ought to be rather than how they actually were. No love, joy or peace came through from this mother to the family because the fruit of the Spirit wasn't realized in her own life. She didn't recognize God's help when she saw it.

The Christian woman needs to learn to live in a real

world, with real problems, with a real God who is capable of meeting our human needs for time and eternity. And she needs to set time against eternity to keep her values straight. In light of eternity much of what we count of supreme worth will be seen as trivia.

A Christian woman gives all she knows of herself to all she knows of God and continues to grow in the knowledge of both. She becomes a channel for the outflow of his character as she takes on "the shape of Christ." She cannot wait for life to change, but says "The life I now live, I live by faith. . . ."

2) We may have an inadequate concept of freedom which makes us afraid to give ourselves completely to anyone, least of all to God. The key to giving ourselves to others is our personal abandonment to God. But we are afraid. And so we hold on tightly to ourselves, afraid to lose our life because we are bent on saving it.

Freedom involves living the way we were intended to live, according to our nature. For instance, a train is constructed to run on rails. It experiences freedom only when it accepts the limitations that its nature imposes on it. A train going along the track at full speed is a wonderful sight, but a train attempting to cross a plowed field is a disaster.

Just so with a pianist who accepts the discipline of the keyboard. Her greatest flights of freedom and self-expression are not in defiance of this discipline, but in submission to it.[2]

Who best knows the nature of our freedom? I would sooner give God that wisdom than claim it for myself. Bishop Frank Houghton once commented that ever since Isaiah had seen the Lord sitting upon a throne, high and lifted up, he had known it was absolutely safe to trust him. Every woman needs that kind of confrontation with God. Only then can she fully abandon herself, and find that in losing her life she saves it. When she lets go and casts herself on the goodness of God, then she will know the meaning of freedom. C. S. Lewis has said, "Until you

---

[2] John R. W. Stott in a lecture *Authority and Freedom.*

have given your self to Him you will not have a real self." She who loses her life shall find it!

A persuaded heart. That is what it means to have faith. And that faith releases "the refreshing energies of God" on our behalf. No position of power, no possessions of this world, no honors or achievements can compare with it. A persuaded heart is a woman's peace and power.